4/13

GOOD JEANS

10 SIMPLE TRUTHS ABOUT FEELING GREAT, STAYING SEXY, AND AGING AGELESSLY

DIANE GILMAN

RUNNING PRESS
PHILADELPHIA · LONDON

ISBN 978-0-7624-4873-9
Library of Congress Control Number: 2012955887

E-book ISBN 978-0-7624-4874-6

9   8   7   6   5   4   3   2   1
Digit on the right indicates the number of this printing

Cover and Interior design by Corinda Cook
Edited by Jennifer Kasius
Cover photography by Bryan Kasm
Typography: Garamond and Bodoni

Running Press Book Publishers
2300 Chestnut Street
Philadelphia, PA 19103-4371

Visit us on the web!
www.runningpress.com

NOTE: The ideas, methods, and suggestions contained in this book are not intended to
replace the advice of a nutritionist, doctor, or other trained health professional. Any changes
to, or additions to, a lifestyle program are at the reader's discretion.

CONTENTS

AGAINST ALL ODDS . . . 7

PART I: DENIM & DIAMONDS (MY STORY) . . . 9

THE TIMES, THEY ARE A-CHANGIN' . . . 10

LIFE BEGINS AT SIXTY . . . 18

AN *ADDAMS-FAMILY* GIRL IN A
LEAVE-IT-TO-BEAVER WORLD . . . 30

IT'S ALL ROCK 'N' ROLL TO ME . . . 41

LOVE IS THE ANSWER . . . 56

THE LOST DECADE . . . 68

PART II:
TEN SIMPLE TRUTHS . . . 83

THE FIRST SIMPLE TRUTH:

IT'S REALLY NOT THAT COMPLICATED.
(So, don't overthink it!) . . . 84

THE SECOND SIMPLE TRUTH:

THE CLASSIC RULEBOOK IS OBSOLETE.
(Toss it!) . . . 106

THE THIRD SIMPLE TRUTH:

YOUR LIFE IS A SELF-PORTRAIT.
(Pick your palette,
lift your brush, start painting.) . . . 124

THE FOURTH SIMPLE TRUTH:

THE UNIVERSE IS LISTENING.
(Don't argue when it answers!) . . . 138

THE FIFTH SIMPLE TRUTH:

SEXUALITY IS LIKE THE PERFECT SOUFFLÉ:
TRICKY BUT DELICIOUS.
(Get the right ingredients.) . . . 152

THE SIXTH SIMPLE TRUTH:

SCIENCE IS A GIRL'S BEST FRIEND.
(Be smart about beautiful.) . . . 170

THE SEVENTH SIMPLE TRUTH:

TECH SAVVY IS THE NEW SEXY.
(Stay plugged into the cosmic conversation.) . . . 184

THE EIGHTH SIMPLE TRUTH:

DARE TO DREAM.
(And watch your dreams come true.) . . . 198

THE NINTH SIMPLE TRUTH:

TIME IS AN ILLUSION.
(Seriously! Ask Einstein!) . . .216

THE TENTH SIMPLE TRUTH:

CHOOSE TO BE THE REAL YOU.
(Become Your "Super Self.") . . . 228

ACKNOWLEDGMENTS . . . 248

AGAINST ALL ODDS

If I told you that everything I ever wanted (and ever wanted to be) happened to me (and for me) after sixty, would you believe me? Career heights I never imagined, the heart-stopping love affair of a lifetime, the beauty, grace, and glamour I'd always dreamed of attaining. Sounds too good to be true, right? Only if you play by the classic rulebook for aging (which I've thrown out). Read my life story and know it can happen to you . . . all you need to do is believe. . . .

PART I:

DENIM & DIAMONDS (MY STORY)

THE TIMES, THEY ARE A-CHANGIN'

In my business, a positive nod from Cathy Horyn, writer for the *New York Times* Fashion & Style section is like a blessing from on high. Any hot young designer would impale herself on a five-inch stiletto for the opportunity to be profiled. So when I heard they wanted to do an article about me and my jeans in July 2012, I was over the moon, but I had three questions:

> **Why?**
>
> *What took them so long?*
>
> **And most important:** *What should I wear?*

Of course, the answer to the first question is money. People in creative industries love to say, "It's not about the money," but if we're honest, that's how most people measure success. One of my favorite sayings is "Money makes blind men see and deaf men hear." So it was gratifying to know that in the mighty mind of the *New York Times* Fashion & Style section, I measure up. My customer base (which feels more like an extended family) is half a million strong. They'll buy $175 million worth of DG2 jeans this year and look fabulous doing it. Those numbers are hard to ignore.

Nonetheless, in this youth-obsessed business (and this youth-obsessed world!), women my age aren't supposed to count for much. We're expected to step out of the mainstream and fade into the wallpaper. Don't even try to suggest otherwise. The evidence is everywhere.

No one can deny my career has survived long beyond the average life span. Which brings me to the second question I asked when I heard that Cathy Horyn wanted to interview me: *What took them so long?* But maybe I should have asked, *What took me so long?*

Wasn't I supposed to be past my prime ten or fifteen years ago? Here I was, sixty-six, achieving greater success and more recoginition than I'd ever known, and about to be profiled in the *New York Times* Fashion & Style section. No one ever told me these would be—or could be—the best years of my life, and if anyone had tried to tell me, chances are, I wouldn't have believed them, because there's so much cosmic noise out there to the contrary.

We are taught (especially as females) from a young age that these are our "declining" (in other words, "throwaway") years. I was frankly astonished when opportunities came flowing out of the universe when I approached sixty, for the simple reason that I was taught the contrary—not only by society, but also in my own household, by a mother who constantly assured me, life for me as a female is over at thirty.

So at the very moment when a career is supposed to be winding down, mine is on fire. At a time when women are supposed to be well past romantic interest, I'm involved in the most sexually and emotionally torrid, fifty-shades-of delicious love affair of my life. My significant other (I'll fondly call him Attila here to protect his privacy) is brilliant, unfairly handsome, almost criminally virile. And he's fourteen years younger than I am. (Be patient. We'll get to the juicy part later.)

At a phase when women are expected to quietly take their place in a rocker on the front porch, retirement is not even a distant dream for me. I'm strutting red carpets in full glam gear, looking and feeling better than I ever have in my life. Which brings us to that all-important third question: *What the you-know-what should I wear to this interview?*

I wanted to look cool and extremely polished, but at the same time, I wanted to be comfortable, to be truly me.

That means jeans.

Jeans are iconic; they capture the essence of femininity, youth, and personality. When you are wearing a perfectly fitting pair of jeans, they say volumes about what you think of yourself and how you take care of yourself. There are a lot of women (including my mother, once upon a time) who feel powerful in a pencil skirt, high heels, and red lipstick, but that's never been me.

I love the look of a successful, cool girl who's not hung up on repping as some super uptight "ladies who lunch" type, so I go for the high-low metaphor of denim and diamonds. The value of a Chanel diamond watch is blazingly obvious, but a great pair of beat-up jeans is just as precious, because the jeans tell a story. They have a rich history, a heritage, a wealth of experience, and a comfortable, sexy sense of self—pair them together, and you've got my favorite true-to-myself look: Denim & Diamonds.

So I went to my *New York Times* Fashion & Style section interview wearing an Alexander McQueen couture jacket, a delicately pleated silk blouse by Chloé, a diamond watch and handbag that are unmistakably Chanel, a pair of insanely dangerous heels (ouch!), and—you guessed it—my trusty DG2 super-skinny, $24 denim jeggings.

I could take that outfit anywhere in the world—from a yacht in Ibiza or Capri in summer, to an outdoor café in Paris, to dinner at a contemporary restaurant in NYC. The language of that outfit is immediately understood and respected. It's a fashion passport that lets you go anywhere. It's easy to comprehend, universal, classy—and in its own relaxed way, sexy!

Cathy Horyn, the reporter who was doing the profile, is a bit of a legend. The *Daily Beast* called her "Fashion's Most Feared Critic." She's been the *Times's* fashion critic since 1999. Before that, she terrified people from a platform at *Vanity Fair*, combining a master's degree in journalism with a California condor's eye for style. She's interviewed everyone from Karl Lagerfeld to Anna Wintour, and she occasionally gets banned from shows by big names like Armani, Carolina Herrera, and Oscar de la Renta. Yes, *banned*.

She's seen every stitch on every runway and pronounced most of it stupid and irrelevant. Just a few weeks before my interview, she'd written in an article about couture culture, in which she said, "The thing is, fashion is a rotten, rotten business. Tough. Full of compromises and shallow values."

Sounds like oodles of fun, huh?

Long story short, there seemed to be nothing anyone could wear that would impress a style tyrant who has the entire fashion world alternately sucking up to her and crying in a corner. There was nothing I could wear that would make her like me, so I just showed up in clothes that made me like myself. The little jeans that could.

I met Cathy Horyn in the iconic ladies-who-lunch café of heavenly Bergdorf Goodman. Like a good little fashionista, I ordered a calorie-scant salad. But as the conversation progressed, I followed it up with a slab of lemon cheesecake. This seemed to surprise her (probably because most of the people she interviews are the circumference of a swizzle stick and would never even sniff a spoon off the dessert cart), but she seemed to appreciate the fact that I ate it because I wanted to, not because it was allowed, or because I needed to prove that I didn't care if it was allowed or not.

To my surprise, I liked her. And she liked me. It was a great interview. (Hardly terrifying at all!) She let me know when she didn't want to go down a particular path, even if it was something I was interested in discussing. She was skillful and knew how to control the pace of the conversation. But as we lingered over a four-hour lunch, I felt comfortable enough to forthrightly ask her why someone who usually writes about the Lagerfeld set was even interested in talking to me.

"I'm the 800-pound gorilla in the fashion room," I said. "We both know I'm in a venue that's not particulary understood or respected by my industry peers. This seems way out in left field for you."

She told me that both the number of jeans I'd sold and the intense reaction from my audience spoke to buying patterns that interested her. The concept of dressing high-low was a big part of our conversation: How it doesn't look right anymore to be head-to-toe couture. We agreed that for us baby boomer women (she's in her late fifties), a pair of jeans with just the right attitude evens the playing field and gives us all the cool of a younger woman without the necessity of virgin abs and low-mileage legs.

When the *Times* profile came out in July 2012, I was thrilled to see that there was only a passing mention of my age. It was all about the business, and since I'm all about the business, I loved that. My age really wasn't relevant to the conversation; she cared about my accomplishments and my fashion philosophy more than anything else.

At one point she actually referred to me as "middle aged," and while I'd like to imagine I'm on track to live til I'm 150, I suspect she thought of me in those terms because I look, feel, and work like most people would expect a woman to look, feel, and work in her forties and fifties.

LIFE BEGINS
AT SIXTY

"What's your secret?" is a question I get a lot. Let me be perfectly clear—it's not a secret—I want to share with all of you what I believe is the essence of of living an AGE-LESS life.

And it's not purely about feeling or looking younger. Human beings do not get younger. I promise you—this is a fact. Google it. You're either aging, or you're dead. But aging doesn't have to mean inevitably going into decline, either. Inspired is not a decade. Healthy is not an age. Beautiful is not a number. Curiosity, sexuality, mental and physical flexibility, optimism, daring to dream—none of these come with term limits. The goal isn't younger; the goal is to be the healthiest, happiest, most radiant human being you can be at any given moment.

That is the essence of aging AGE-LESS.

When we make that shift—in both vocabulary and mindset—we breathe into being an entirely new vision of the second half of life. Every day is a movable feast of opportunity; every opportunity is primed with a wealth of experience; and every experience takes on a delicious piquancy, a preciousness that we were just too damn dumb to see or feel when we were in our twenties.

Through the call-in segments on my television shows and my *Huffington Post* (HuffPo) blog, I constantly hear from middle aged women who are longing for mind-expanding work, earth-moving love, foundation-rocking sex, and soul-grabbing purpose. They've been taught to believe that those ships have sailed. But I believe women can unlearn these negative messages and embrace a new way of thinking.

During television shows in both the United States and Europe, I talk to as many viewers as possible. These are the women who've created the wave that caught Cathy Horyn's attention. Each one means a lot to me, but every once in a while, a particular caller will grab ahold of my heart.

Chatting with a caller on an evening show not long ago, I caught tears in her voice when she said, "I want to put this simply. Thank you for giving *me* back to *me*."

It seems crazy that a pair of jeans could make that much of a difference in someone's life, but I knew immediately what she meant. So many of us lose the essence of who we are when we reach this transitional period called middle age. Suddenly, our body, face, energy level, libido—everything that adds up to our sense of our female self—aren't *us* anymore. We look in the mirror and see a stranger. (Like Bella confronting her "older self" in *Twilight*.)

Worst of all, we blame ourselves. So many of us women step into the fitting room at a store that caters to twentysomethings, and when the jeans don't fit, we don't see the jeans as wrong, we see ourselves as wrong.

Quite frankly, this is bull. The reality is (hope you're sitting down for this), before menopause, women age half as fast as men. After, they age *five* times faster. What's to feel guilty about there? That's science, genetics, Mother Nature—not a lack of willpower or some kind of deep personal failing. So stop beating yourself up about the passage of time—start to work with it instead.

"I'm not looking to be twenty again," another caller told me, "but your jeans make me 'look like how I feel'. I'm sixty, and now I believe how I feel inside is how I look outside. My life is back in harmony."

Harmony. Denim and diamonds.

Exactly like a perfect pair of jeans, we've reached just the right fade. We speak that universal language: class, grace, experience. A twenty-five-year-old woman has plenty of assets we don't have, but she can't fake, buy, implant, or paint on wisdom, personal style, and richness of character. It takes decades to create what we've got. But it takes focus and effort to make the most of it. To enjoy it! To use it to our advantage. And to share it.

Because I'm in fashion, my face is always buried in the editorial pages of magazines. As I've gotten older, and the models have gotten younger, I felt more and more marginalized by the very culture that my generation created.

However, a few recent breakthroughs suggest there's a revolution on the way. In January 2012, when I first saw Meryl Streep on the cover of *Vogue*, I said, *At last! One of my own kind!* This was monumental. Revolutionary! The Berlin Wall of ageism was crumbling. We're talking *Vogue*, people: the biggest, snobbiest, most powerful high-fashion magazine in the world. At sixty-two, Streep was the oldest cover model in the magazine's history, and where *Vogue* goes, our culture follows.

Even before that, we saw a younger—(but only by a

decade)—Madonna on the cover of December 2011's *Harper's Bazaar*—a major "I'll have what she's having" moment. (Whatever she's doing, eating, chanting, injecting, or abstaining from is definitely working.) In her mid-fifties, she is every bit the powerhouse she was back in her torpedo-bra days, which is an amazing feat, because aging in the public eye is such a minefield—you're always one collagen injection away from being one of David Letterman's punch lines.

Candidly, we saw both these women poised and ready to lose their way, and then, find themselves again.

Meryl, ever the good girl, believed that she would be forced to pack it in when she turned forty, which is equal to eighty in Hollywood. The year she turned fifty, she was offered three movies—all casting her as a witch. As she told *Vogue,* she turned to her husband and said: "Well, what should we do? Because it's over."

Instead of giving up, though, she did the impossible. She plowed through limited ideas of what a "middle aged" woman can be (in show business) with utter intelligence. She survived in Hollywood, and against all odds, even thrived. Since then, she's done everything from sexy rom-coms to the screen adaptation of a Broadway musical, and more than half of her Oscar nominations have been earned since she turned forty. (Up yours, Hollywood youth worshippers.)

Meryl came into her own as she aged, with a classy, natural, authentic appearance. No trout lips or frozen brows here. She looks healthy, vibrant, knowing, strong, mature, and comfortable.

Most importantly—and, I believe, the real key to her success—she never shut down. She always understood her strength, which is her ability as an actress to effortlessly access and honestly convey her emotions. To do so, she has had to open her heart, again and again, and have the courage to be very exposed. That fearlessness is a major key for all of us to aging AGE-LESS.

Madonna, a bad-girl savant, awkwardly clutched onto her youth a little too long, then relocated her trailblazing balls and basically flipped society the bird with her bangin' body, bold career choices, and hot young boyfriends.

Every woman goes through a transitional period as she ages, after which many end up off-center, lost, and less than true to themselves. Some never find their way out of the woods. (I'll be telling you all about my dark "lost decade" and emergence into the "light" later in the book.) We desperately need sexy, sophisticated, and confident mature women role models in our media—*real* women, not Frankenstein constructs—showing us that it is possible to redefine aging.

"To have fun, that's the main issue," Madonna says in her *Harper's Bazaar* profile. "To continue to be a provocateur, to do what we perceive as the realm of young people, to provoke, to be rebellious, to start a revolution."

Mission accomplished. These two magazine covers signal the beginning of a long-overdue media and retail insurrection.

Baby boomer women are the larger half of the biggest generational population on the planet, and so far, we're the biggest missed opportunity in retail history. When we need a great little dress for a special occasion, we show up at the store with cash in hand, but ninety-nine percent of the rack space screams, *twentysomethings only!* We are the invisible woman!

Let's take this thinking a step further: Viagra's been raking in billions for fourteen years. In their television ads, it's always some silver fox with a hot blond at his side. And there's still no female-enhancing counterpart! What message are we supposed to get from that? Our sexuality is expendable? We should just put on a baggy, "hide me" dress and catch the next ice floe out of town?

"I find whenever someone writes anything about me, my age is right after my name," says Madonna. "It's almost like they're saying, 'Here she is, but remember she's this age, so she's not that relevant anymore.'"

That's been the attitude, from Hollywood Boulevard to Fashion Avenue. Many of us, including me have found the path through middle age to be "the Boulevard of Broken Dreams." But in greater numbers every day, we're resisting that attitude *with attitude*.

I encouraged everyone I knew to buy a thousand copies of that *Vogue* issue with Meryl on the cover. I wanted to make it the most popular cover ever and send a message back to advertisers and editors: We are here, and the biggest mistake you could make in this economy would be to continue to marginalize us and judge us by our age instead of our buying power. The Silver Tsunami has started, and it is unstoppable.

When somebody gives you a hand up, helps you rediscover the essence of who you are, it's life-changing. I know, because before he died, my life partner, Jim, did just that for me (much more about Jim later). He cared enough to be honest, to challenge me, to inspire me. Early on, I made it my mission to pay that forward and be a champion for those women who were being cut from the pack and brought to their knees by aging, as so many of us are after a certain age—it has become my life's mission.

But I didn't realize any of this until I had pulled myself out of my "lost decade" at age fifty-nine and came to a personal space where I saw that I would have to build the stage on which I wanted to play out this part of my life. It was within my power—and only prudent—for me to create the setting, cast the characters, and design the set and costumes. Confronted with big and small questions about how to do that, I settled into a learning process that will last the rest of my life. There are no easy answers, and we all have to be responsible for discovering and sticking to what works for us. But I have figured out a few universal truths that really work for me, and I suspect you and I have a lot in common, even though it might not look that way on the surface. So, I'm betting they'll work for you, too.

Always remember this: You are not alone! We are not alone! There are tens of thousands of us baby boomer women out there wishing for a better quality of life and a way back to vibrancy and joy—but with no idea how of to get there or even where to start—or that it's possible.

I know because I was one of them—lost in the vast and lonely sea of aging, alone in a tiny rowboat with no oars or rudder to steer back to shore—until not so long ago. Because I did find my way back, I'm now in the amazing position of being able to share my experience with all of you.

So many of you are telling me exactly how you feel and what you want. You want change! You want to feel important! You want sex! You want to feel sexy! You want love! You want comfort! You want to matter to the conversation at large— in your bedroom, in your home, in your workplace, in your community! If anyone knows how to rally a group around an important issue of the day and create real change, baby boomers do!

Another important component of our journey is this: Find a sense of shared experience. Isolation can be a major ager, and it can make issues seem larger than they really are. Unity looks so different today from the sixties love-in vibe—now it's a global community—it's Facebook—it's the Internet Twitter minutia—it's the cosmic conversation so essential for staying relevant.

So find a way to get out there and engage in some level of group conversation. In the New York City fashion world, where I live, it's all about the urban, cool-girl fashionista. It's very "fast"—it's very visual—but if you're sending out the right "vibe," you're in the club, no matter your age.

What I see there these days is actually very encouraging. When you are truly cool—like Karl Lagerfield, chief designer of Chanel, who's well into his eighties—age is irrelevant (the central message of this book).

In the coming chapters, I'll share with you my life story and the invaluable lessons I've learned along the way, and I'll invite you to ask yourself some tough questions. (Chances are, the answers are already patiently waiting—but hiding—in your heart.) I'll also discuss a revolutionary idea: All it takes is a commitment to change one thing, and you'll be on your way to a new way of thinking and a whole new, reenergized life.

I won't pretend to have all the answers, but I consider it a privilege to share what I do know!

Of all the truths I've gathered through my experience, one remains immutable: As long as we're alive, meaningful change is possible. There's a great line in the movie *Vanilla*

Sky: "Every passing minute is another chance to turn it all around." Welcome to my world!

I'm living proof of that! So maybe I should start by sharing my own unique story.

AN *ADDAMS-FAMILY* GIRL IN A *LEAVE-IT-TO-BEAVER* WORLD

The end of World War II ushered in a dismal fashion era for the American Everywoman. Anyone who adores the torturous crinolines and bullet bras on *Mad Men* more than likely never had to wear them. Only women with a specific body type looked good. I certainly didn't fit that profile.

I was born in Beverly Hills in 1945 and evolved into a chubby, pale, freckled, child with a wild mane of insanely curly hair, which my mother endeavored to tame. I was miserable when she cropped Mamie Eisenhower bangs on the front of my head and fried them into submission with a curling iron every morning. I couldn't wait to get to school so I could duck into the girls' bathroom and drench the front of my head in the sink, my best attempt to restore something of a natural order to those poor little bangs.

I despised the constricting pencil skirts, boxy coats, and rained-out colors of the fifties. They felt foreign and drab to me, and they said nothing to me about who I really was or wanted to be. Even as a little girl, I somehow knew that I was destined to live an extraordinary life. I wanted everything to be colorful, magical, and remarkable, and when I grew up enough to attach a specific vision to that longing and desire, I absolutely knew I wanted to spend my life designing fashion in glamorous New York City—quite a leap of faith for a girl from the small desert town of Whittier, California, where my family lived from when I was ages nine to seventeen.

One of my earliest childhood memories is of being about five years old and standing in the market, gazing at the current issue of *Seventeen*. On the cover, a headline read: *A Teenage Model's Weekend in New York*. Below it, Colleen Corby wore a chic red coat and a black tam, and the New York City skyline behind her featured the same iconic buildings I now see from my living room window.

That's me, I immediately knew. *That's going to be my life.*

This free-spirited fashion model in New York struck a

chord of familiarity within me in a way that no other image set before me ever had. I don't remember relating to one single role model among the middle aged women I saw as I grew up. The older women on television were self-deprecating comedians like Lucille Ball; frumpy caricatures like Andy Griffith's Aunt Bea; a crabapple teacher on *Dobie Gillis*; or some stereotypical witch like Agnes Moorehead as Endora on *Bewitched*. Older women in fashion magazines? Nonexistent! That would have been like seeing a pink elephant in a tutu on the cover of *Vogue*.

In real life, the older women I saw in my neighborhood were exactly who they were supposed to be, according to folkways: soft-bodied dowagers who gave their lives to their families, slid gently but swiftly downhill to the rocking chair, and never made a fuss about what they wanted for their own lives. That's how aging was defined for little girls of my generation, while little boys had Gregory Peck and Cary Grant to emulate.

My mother had impeccable style and was an experienced seamstress. Perfect environment for an aspiring designer to flourish, right?

Wrong.

Not only did she not teach me to sew, but sewing was strictly forbidden. She associated her own sewing with the misery that befell her family during the Great Depression. The huge mansion she grew up in became a boarding house, and she, like a humbled princess, was forced to be the boardinghouse maid, cleaning, cooking, and sewing clothes for herself and her seven siblings until her early thirties, when my father rented a room from her family and then rescued her from being an old maid.

I can see now that my mother was different from many women during that time—not satisfied by being a mother, she longed to be an architect and seemed to want so much more, but she could never get at it. Looking back, I understand that she took her dissatisfaction out on me. At the time, I just knew that she always seemed to be frustrated with her life, and most particularly, with me.

Sewing, in her mind, was forced, menial labor. She had a little Singer machine in a carrying case at home, but that was just for repairing girdles (remember those?), bras, and silk stockings, which she did obsessively, even though my father was a successful jeweler. The Great Depression was the gash in her emotional memory. No matter how affluent they became, she would always be fixated on frugality. She used that sewing machine but hated it because she associated it with humiliating poverty.

And designing clothes—well, who ever heard of a normal person doing that? It was artsy and odd and associated with loose morals! No sane, decent woman expected to have an extraordinary career back then—or actually, any career at all. The phrase "career woman" wasn't even coined until many years later. My mother's plan was for me to be a kindergarten teacher—if I absolutely insisted on working—and to marry a doctor, dentist, or lawyer—no discussion, no debate.

Rebellious and determined, I used to sneak the sewing machine under my bed in the middle of the night. I taught myself how to sew, using one hand to push the foot pedal and the other to guide the fabric. It was quiet enough that I could sometimes get away with sewing for a few hours. Not always, though. When I was discovered, I was beaten, but I couldn't stop myself. Even at that age, design wasn't a "hobby" or an "interest" for me; it was a spiritual calling, a compulsion, a necessity. It was as much a part of me then as it is now. I don't think I could have stopped if I tried, and I didn't try, despite my mother's unbridled rage. I already knew that designing was my destiny and that sewing was part of the learning curve, and I was determined to pursue both of them.

I had a lot to fight against, including an unforgettable and powerfully destructive statement my mother used to make: "A woman's life is over at thirty." Seriously? Oh yes, she meant it! As far as she was concerned, you'd better do everything meaningful in your female life—fall in love, marry, bear children—before then, because afterward, no one would want you!

No coincidence, I think, that when my mother was in her mid-thirties (an "old maid" in that day) she had married my father, a deeply disturbed man who sexually abused and beat me from my earliest childhood memories. From the age of three, I was in survival mode, desperately trying to find ways to do the normal things that other kids took for granted, like taking a bath by myself, without him in it.

One particular incident is seared into my nightmares. I was eight and trying to get away from my father. He came after me with a butcher knife, and I darted into the bathroom, locking the door as he raged and pounded. Finally, everything went quiet, like in the eye of the storm. I remained there, perfectly still for what seemed like an eternity, trying to think how to get out. Then I looked up and saw his distorted face in the mirror. I was terrified. He was trying to get in the window!

How could a man do that to his own child? How could a mother allow that to go on and years later be angry at the child for being the cause of the fighting in the house? What manner of parental brain could conjure up these horrifying scenarios? It took me decades—literally—to let go of the resentment, anger, and sorrow I carried out of my childhood, but even now, the thought of that face in the mirror twists my stomach into a knot.

When I refused to cooperate with my father's abuse as a teen, and I was finally big enough to fight back, he tried to have me committed to a mental institution, saying I was rebellious, unbalanced, out of control. In fact, I was driven, focused, ambitious, and intelligent. I approached my future with singular vision and galvanized purpose. A normal set of upper-middle-class Jewish parents would have nurtured all that, been proud of it, but that wasn't the household I grew up in. My parents had very narrow points of view about what my life path should be. There was no discussion or debate; I wasn't invited to insert my own vision. I was expected to be mute, submissive, and numb, and go into the life they chose for me, an alien life that would have been nothing I wanted and everything I hated.

My exit from our impossibly dysfunctional home was abrupt and ugly, a tipping point at which years of abuse and violence ripped apart at the seam.

When I was eighteen or nineteen, I was in my second year at UCLA, where I lived in a sorority house, thankfully away from home. I thought sororities were so stupid, but my parents had made me join because that was their idea of what young women were supposed to be. Even though I was in college, I was still very much under their control. One night, I came downstairs at their house, dressed to go out on a date. I'd designed and made a backless pinafore dress for the occasion—deep red velvet to match my date's red Corvette. I knew this guy was gay. It was obvious! We were on our way out for a purely innocent evening of fun and music.

With this poor kid looking on, horrified and dumbstruck, my mother shrieked, "You look like a slut! That dress belongs in the gutter."

She seized the front of my dress and ripped it off me, leaving me humiliated, standing there in my underwear, dress in shreds. My mortified friend shot me a sympathetic look and beat a hasty retreat. I ran to my room, locked the door, and cried for hours.

When I finally gathered the courage to leave the house, my father again threatened me with a butcher knife. But I wasn't a child anymore. This time, when he threw the knife at me, I grabbed it and threw it back, catching his hand against the kitchen counter. He bellowed after me, stunned and enraged, as I ran.

I hopped into my VW Bug and sped off into the night. Later that same night, driving around L.A. with some girlfriends, I got pulled over. The cops found a tiny stub of a joint in my car, an amount I can't imagine would even be a misdemeanor today. Back then it was enough to get me arrested. I had to spend the night in jail. Even worse, the next morning, I had to face my parents, who bailed me out—after much begging—with my own money, I might add.

As I sat in the back seat of their Cadillac on the drive home, they announced the new status quo. I would be forced to move home. They were going to have my two dogs killed (yes, my parents actually said this to me). They were going to throw out all of my clothes. They were going to listen in on and monitor all of my phone conversations going forward. They were going to find me a husband, whom I would marry as arranged. End of story. End of problem with their rebellious child.

By this point, I knew enough to pretend to go along with them. I thanked them for their caring, casually asked what was for dinner, and then, when we got home, I told them I just needed to go for a little drive to clear my head before dinner, silently praying they would let me walk out that front door. I have no idea why, but they actually gave me the keys. I drove away in my VW Bug, with maybe a dime in my pocket, and I never saw my parents again for thirty-five years.

Long story short, I grew up in *The Addams Family* when everything on television was *Leave It to Beaver* and *Father Knows Best*. My template for life was about fighting my way through things. With the dark legacy of all that—plus my mother's powerlessness (or selective blindness)—hell yes, I was rebellious. But I was a rebel with a cause. Crafting my own destiny was not an option; it was imperative to my survival.

I had to rebel against these two people who should never have had a child; nothing about my family intermingled or meshed in any healthy way. I had to rebel to survive, but beyond that, I knew I could never live the life that they dictated. As a twentysomething, I knew I couldn't live the life that society dictated, either. It wasn't going to be about being a teacher and marrying a doctor. It was going to be all about being free—free to pursue my destiny!

Thank god for the sixties!

IT'S ALL ROCK 'N' ROLL TO ME

I was in college the first time I saw Janis Joplin. A talent agent I was dating called me one night and said, "Come to Whiskey a Go Go on the Sunset Strip. I need to see this new act."

Because I was still living in a sorority house with a strict ten p.m. curfew, this was a bit tricky, but where there's a will there's a way, and I was never short on will. I carefully removed the slats from the kitchen window and catapulted out to the lawn. A little while later, I was standing right by the stage at the Whiskey a Go Go, which was usually closed to the public on Monday nights but had opened for this special performance. I was there with about twenty other agents and their ladies, a small, intimate group of industry insiders about to witness something absolutely extraordinary.

Janis stumbled into the spotlight, a bottle of Southern Comfort swinging in her hand, wild hair looking like she'd just stepped out of a tornado. She opened her mouth, and it was electric. That moment crystallized everything I ever wanted from life. For someone raised in a repressed household, the idea that you could be a woman and be that free, that full of power, was nothing short of mind-blowing.

I suddenly realized that no one had the power or authority to hold me back. I always knew I had an innate talent for design. Even when I was a little girl cobbling clothes together with the sewing machine under my bed, I had singular faith in one thing: I'm good at this. No amount of beating or berating could convince me otherwise.

Hell, even when I was about two years old, I picked up a crayon and drew a stick figure and colored in a polka-dot dress. The die was cast at a very young age.

That night, I looked up and saw this stunning, wild woman—tarnished but brilliant, raw but accomplished, a true original—taking full possession of her own power to do what she was meant to do. She'd been laughed out of her hometown and told she wasn't even good enough to sing in her high school choir. She went out and built her life from the ground up, bigger and bolder than anyone would have imagined. She let it all hang loose that night at the Whiskey, and it was like a battle cry: Be what you want. Be who you were meant to be!

It was 1965, and when I heard about her death just five years later, I was devastated. The tragedy was that she succumbed to the idea that drugs could free a person from pain, when as far as I was concerned, she had already freed herself from the outmoded ideas of what a woman should be and bared her true soul to the world in her music, dress, and everything about her. She had no role model. Back then, role models were Jackie O. and Grace Kelly. Janis and I were simply not the hair-sprayed-bouffant-flip and pencil-skirt type. She became an inspirational role model for me, but also a cautionary tale.

It's still thrilling to think how unbelievably revolutionary everything in the sixties was. We baby boomers raised a voice, a rallying cry heard round the world.

I'm in my sixties now, but I still have the same head on my shoulders that I had in my twenties. I never fail to get excited about traveling, creating, styling, and expressing myself artistically.

But I miss that sense of generational camaraderie we once shared. In fact, I find it sad how dispersed and isolated we've become. We were the generation that celebrated the individual within the unified whole. We've always been a proud and loud generation. We were music, fashion, politics, culture. We were originals! We faced up to hard truths at home and abroad, and tried to effect change. We did change the world. Then, one by one, we left the group to form families and adult lives. And as we aged, I think we feared we weren't relevant anymore. We grew silent. We grew isolated. There's no power in that!

We need to come back together again. Where are the rabble-rousers and sit-ins and love-ins?

Sometimes I want to throw open the window and say, "Wake up!" This is a whole new world. Everything our parents and the government said and promised is going by the wayside. The old view of the gold watch at fifty-five—forget that; middle age doesn't even begin until sixty or sixty-five now! Some now say most baby boomers will work until we're eighty. (I'm counting on it!) We'll need a whole new kind of support, a whole new source of energy. We'll need to rediscover that battle cry within ourselves and redefine what striding (not limping) into old age means.

That night at the legendary Whiskey a Go Go on the

Sunset Strip, I put my finger on a specific overriding desire that had always been in my life and always will be: I wanted to create and experience one extraordinary moment after another.

The rise of the hippies was a delicious hello for me. These were my people! We were radicals, rockers, true originals, turn-this-shit-inside-outers. We were the first generation of women to wear jeans and the first generation of men to find that sexy. We kidnapped denim from down on the farm and turned it into an art form. Then we kidnapped the farm and turned it into Woodstock.

Jeans were my entrée into the world of rock stars. Around 1965, after I left UCLA, I opened a little boutique across from Canter's Delicatessen on Fairfax Avenue in L.A. with a collective of girlfriends. It was called I'm a Hog for You Baby, which we had determined was the first rock-'n'-roll song. We hardly had any money, so all we could afford were simple racks along the walls. But we painted the walls acid green and neon orange, and we stocked the racks with A-line dresses that I'd designed and sewed in different treatments and fabrics. Our hook was that every dress in the store cost ten dollars.

One day, a beautiful, white Rolls-Royce pulled up out front, and Cher sailed in. She never said a word, just surveyed the merchandise, and with a characteristic swish of her long black hair, she pushed the door open and crowed out, "Sonny!"

Sonny Bono and the chauffer, apparently accustomed to the drill, trudged in and were ordered to carry out literally every single dress we had—about 200 in total—and loaded them into the trunk of the Rolls, leaving my friends and me utterly speechless and absolutely thrilled—but completely out of merchandise. We had to close the store for five days while I manically sewed more dresses so we could reopen.

I had already started painting, crafting, slashing, enhancing, and creating unique statement jeans when I was just a teenager, and for the first time, positive reinforcement flowed in my direction. Soon I was creating one-of-a-kind jeans for rock stars, including Cher, Janis Joplin, the members of Jefferson Airplane, and Jimi Hendrix in L.A. and San Francisco—those were the golden years of rock 'n' roll.

When Janis Joplin kicked back to Texas and flipped the bird to everyone who looked down on her in high school, she was wearing the jeans I'd embroidered with sixties floral designs. Jimi Hendrix wore the jeans I'd embellished with suede fringe and Native American beading as he jammed with his fellow stoners at after-parties and impromptu park concerts. Grace Slick and her Jefferson Airplane bandmates cruised Haight-Ashbury in my jeans.

For me, jeans were self-expression, rebellion, youth, freedom, the ultimate "cool." During my bleak high school years, I'd been forced to kneel in the hallway at school to show that my regulation skirt was long enough. When it wasn't—which was often—I was forced to walk home and change into a longer skirt. Jeans were strictly forbidden. So when we broke free from these outmoded rules and started wearing jeans, it was about finding what fit us instead of forcing ourselves to fit some stodgy style dictated by society. But above all else, my jeans were *me*.

Not surprisingly, considering my childhood, I found it difficult to make deep personal connections with people, especially men. In a pattern typical of an abusive household, I chose men who were the far opposite of my father. I wasn't interested in anyone who wasn't unpredictable and hard to figure out—I was only interested in the ultimate Bad Boys. There was the radio DJ, the drug dealer, and the biker—anything but the conservative my father had been. (Thank God, I eventually realized that a man could be extraordinary without being destructive.)

My refuge, my comfort, my one tried and true, then and now, has always been my talent in design. It was my sanctuary, my safe room, my sacred place that no one could take away from me, and I quickly discovered that it would take me everywhere I wanted to go.

Not that I got there right away. First, I got myself out of the sorority house and moved to Topanga Canyon, the heart of all that was bohemian and free in those days. It was truly a wild time. Everything was accepted, and anything was possible. The unbelievable happened every day.

One night, I was at a decadent, endless dinner at Frank Zappa's house in Laurel Canyon. The wine and weed were flowing free, and everyone was feeling groovy.

"Now all we need is for a longhaired dwarf to come out from under the tablecloth and say he's been living under there," I remarked in an offhand way.

As if on cue, a little person with a wild mane of hair and

waist-length beard emerged and said he lived under the table. That's just how life was back then.

After about two years, in 1967, the clothing collective dissolved, and our shop closed. For a while I bummed around Europe with Deep Purple, feeling utterly free in my bangin' rocker chick jeans, with my bangin' rocker chick body, and my twentysomething "screw you, establishment" invincibility.

About a year after the shop closed, I went to San Francisco with a jazz musician I'd been living with. Even though I'd been free from my parents for several years, I'd never felt entirely at ease in L.A.—I was always looking over my shoulder. I was glad to put some more distance between us.

Then, after the jazz musician faded out of the picture, I lived in San Francisco (rather unhappily) with a well-known rock-'n'-roll DJ—the exhilarating life of endless rock star parties, concerts and backstage passes was fun, but I knew I didn't really have a connection with the guy.

Even more than that, I'd never shaken that craving for the place I'd always known was my true home, the place

I'd seen myself conquering ever since I caught a glimpse of the mod life of that fabulous teenage model on the cover of *Seventeen*.

So, how did I get to Manhattan? Well, do you believe in karma? In fate? I didn't at that point. Until I had a vivid dream one night that profoundly changed my life.

The dream was about an attractive guy I'd known in college—we'll call him "Cool Boy"—and it was so real, so compelling that I felt I had to find him, to see him. I called a mutual friend who was living in San Francisco and asked, "Whatever happened to that guy?"

Our friend in common said, "So strange of you to ask. He just flew into L.A. to pick up his master's degree!"

Okay, people, whatever your belief system is, you must admit: that was an amazing coincidence, at the very least. Personally, I've never been one to ignore it when the universe posts a giant billboard in front of me—even back then, when I didn't yet know what I believed.

I got our friend to put Cool Boy on a flight to San Francisco. We met up later that day, and by the end of the evening, we were packed and on a flight to New York City, where we lived together for almost a decade.

I got off that airplane in late 1971/early 1972, a college dropout in my mid-twenties, hoping to find a job in the fashion industry, but of course, that didn't happen. It quickly sank in that, without a conventional design education, none of the venerable fashion institutions would take a chance on me.

To pay the rent, I got a night job waiting tables at Max's Kansas City, the infamous hangout of Andy Warhol and his crew of characters. I always hated that job. The other waitresses were so mean to me, and it constantly blew me away what drugged-up messes most of the people in Warhol's circle were. I went to a few parties at the Factory, and it was this whole dark drug culture. He was the evil ringmaster—always observing but never participating. It was almost like he enjoyed watching the people around him destroy themselves.

I didn't have time for that. In fact, it frightened me. I had a mission. New York was hypercompetitive compared to San Francisco. I realized that I was going to have to become much more professional and toughen up to break into fashion. I knew I didn't want to be a stylist for rock-'n'-roll bands— I wanted a much broader venue and audience—and so I got even more serious about creating my own designs.

I had to start somewhere, so I got a day job at Bloomingdale's, miserably selling old-lady "foundations" and bullet bras—way before Madonna made them fashionable—alongside middle aged saleswomen in molded rubber sandals. And then . . . nothing happened. I was beginning to think maybe Seventh Avenue was going to become my "boulevard of broken dreams." Still, I read *Women's Wear Daily* like it was my Bible, and I saved every spare penny and used every stolen moment to design, cut, and sew my own mini fashion collection.

I've heard luck defined as "preparedness meeting opportunity." I didn't know it at the time, but I was preparing for one of the luckiest breaks of my life.

One day at Bloomie's, I was helping the store's fashion director rearrange my department floor space, when I mentioned that I designed clothes. *You and everyone else in New York*—I could see her internally rolling her eyes. But she gave me an appointment—even if it was two months later.

When it came time for the meeting, I showed the woman everything I had. Wow! She loved my designs! On the spot, Bloomie's bought $100,000 worth of my clothing. Sounds too good to be true—like the stuff of every young designer's fantasies, right? Not really—I actually, literally, burst into tears when I realized I didn't have the money to fill such a huge order.

To my utter shock, and undying gratitude, in 1978, Bloomingdale's offered to fund everything—including a series of centerfold ads in the Sunday edition of the *New York Times*—and they put my designs in every window of their 59th Street flagship store. I was stunned, speechless (for once), and thrilled.

Just like that, the good people at Bloomie's legitimized my talent and launched my career as a New York designer. Little did I know it at the time, but that position in the foundations department was the last job I would ever have working for someone else. Forever forward, for better or for worse, I would be my own boss.

The only way I can describe this turn of events is to say that it was the fashion industry equivalent of the understudy being flung into the spotlight when the Broadway star breaks a leg on opening night. It was that random, that magical, that serendipitous—and that life-changing.

In my early thirties, I was generating my clothes, my way, and loving it. No more bullet bras by day; no more slinging drinks by night. Instead, my days consisted of executing my passion for design.

And not only that, but also, I was doing something I'd always wanted to do, *for myself*, while most designers my age had to create their designs under someone else's name and vision.

I was no working stiff, though. It was the fabulous disco era of Studio 54. I loved the music, the fashion, the glittering nightlife. I was friends with a group of flamboyant gay guys, one of whom drove a white Rolls-Royce with an interior lined in white mink (really!). We would just pull up and park it on the sidewalk in front of Studio 54, trail in nonchalantly—looking quite glam—and dance the night away. It was a seriously fantastic time; every night was the perfect excuse to go all out. Drag queens, stars, gorgeous gay men, and seriously beautiful women, all looking so glamorous, flirting and strutting and twirling through this room paved in scarlet carpet. Every night at two a.m., a giant cutout of the man in the moon would descend from the ceiling, a spoon to his nose, and sparkle dust would sprinkle down and blanket the dance floor.

The first night I was there, so innocent and naïve and slightly overwhelmed, I soon had to pee. I fought my way across the crowded lounge and went into the ladies' room. Only there were pairs of men's feet in almost all of the stalls. Panicky, confused, I thought I'd made a mistake and apologized to no one in particular as I darted into what I soon realized was the men's room, which of course, was more of the same. Everywhere were these endless lines of cocaine laid out on the black shelves that lined the bathroom walls. People were having sex, shooting up, doing all manner of insane things. It was quite an education, and I had a lot to learn—I was thirty-four.

Every night it was a midnight supper, Studio 54, the Roxy, after-hour clubs, and breakfast at dawn. Then it was go home to take a shower, maybe take a one-hour nap, then go to work, come home to sleep a few more hours, get up, rifle through my wardrobe, get dressed, and go out all over again.

Studio 54 was such a gorgeous, incandescent bubble, and even when we were in the midst of it, just floating along, twirling endlessly on the dance floor while Donna Summer sang "Last Dance," we knew it had to burst at some point. But not quite yet. I was on top of the world, doing the work I loved by day and partying like a movie star at night—and yet, something was missing.

LOVE IS
THE ANSWER

Jim Rush was a once-celebrated college football player with a blind eye, enormous heart, and ancient soul. No one watching him barrel through a defensive line on the football field would have anticipated that his football career would give way to his greater purpose as a holistic counselor, but by the time he came into my life, the bulldozer hustle of football had given way to a profoundly gentle ministry.

While he was still playing for UCLA, soon after the Los Angeles Rams had recruited him, he had been standing on a porch one day when it collapsed beneath him. He lost an eye, ending his dream of a football career. Instead of perceiving this as a tragedy, he came to accept that it was his vehicle for becoming the person he was meant to be. He would go on to teach me the importance of always staying open to everything that happens and staying true to oneself, no matter how devastating it might seem at the time—like how I never would have found my true destiny in television if I hadn't lost the right to design under my own name for several agonizing years. But more about that later.

I would never have found Jim in the first place if things hadn't gotten dark in my own life around that time. Drugs were everywhere in New York, especially in the club scene, but the man I'd moved there with—Cool Boy—had diverged from a good-time guy into serious addiction.

It's always been a strength of mine that I've been able to turn around and walk away whenever things started to get too destructive. Maybe it comes from my childhood and my ability to escape from my parents and their negative home environment and oppression.

It wasn't easy to leave him, though, as Cool Boy had become my business partner. Plus, when I began to distance myself from him and the drugs that he made a way of everyday life, I lost most of my friends who shared his same lifestyle. But I knew it had to happen.

Afterward, I was living—alone now—and working in a big loft on 14th Street, way before the Meat Packing District became cool. One night, a man I knew by sight from Studio 54 followed me home, broke in, beat me up, and held me hostage for hours in a drug-fueled rage. It was Memorial Day weekend. My neighbors were all out of town, and so for what seemed like an eternity, no one heard me screaming for help. Finally, when he passed out, I escaped. I was cut, bruised, bleeding, and traumatized, and I had to go to the hospital. I looked so bad—disheveled and frightening—that no taxi driver would stop for me, so I limped my way to the nearest hospital emergency room.

After being patched up, I flew to a tropical island for a week to recuperate. On my way home, in the little island airport, a complete stranger approached me.

"Beware," he said. "You're going to be followed home on a holiday weekend, and this time, the guy is going to kill you."

Talk about jarring! After what had just happened to me, I was understandably freaked out. I didn't want to hear anymore. But he persisted.

"I'm just trying to save you," he said. "I know this is going to happen to you, and you're going to die."

Finally, I called airport security to drag the guy away and never saw him again, but I couldn't get his words out of my mind. Was this prophecy? Could it really happen again? Back in New York, I mentioned my fears to my hairdresser. She told me about a very empathetic man she knew who worked as a spiritual advisor and could possibly help me. That was Jim.

In the beginning, ours was a working relationship. I realized at some point, I had deep wounds that were never going to heal without help. Jim recognized my problems without prejudice and showed me how to get past anger and bitterness. He emotionally detoxed and purified me with hard work and compassionate therapy. From there, we became friends. I suppose he was a bit of a father figure, twelve years my senior, but above all else, he was Jim, and he became my confidant, my safe haven—my defender and protector.

Jim was doing seminars and seeing individual clients, but at some point, he was displaced from his apartment for reasons I don't recall. I had never gone back to that 14th Street apartment, and I was now living in a huge loft in SoHo—before it was SoHo. One night he asked if he could stay. I said yes, and he stayed for eighteen years.

Our day-to-day existence together was that string of extraordinary experiences that I'd always hoped my life would be. We talked at length about physics and metaphysics, the boundless energy of life beyond life. I savored every word like it was a gourmet feast.

I'd had a couple of big successes at that point in my career. The Cabal blouse—which had an old-fashioned, prairie air and big, 1890's, leg-of-mutton sleeves—was so wildly popular that I did it in all kinds of fabrics for years, including washable silks, which were a total sensation. At one point in the early nineties, there was a season when my designs were in every window of every department store in Manhattan at the same time—but success was always followed by fallow periods, in which I wasn't able to come up with the next big design that would connect with people. I struggled. There was no consistency. I didn't realize it at the time, but I just wasn't mature enough to be truly focused until the moment in my life when I designed for myself and my fellow baby boomer sisters.

I learned so much from Jim. He taught me how to access the positive energy within myself and let it shine through in my work. I always said that before I met Jim, I was like a lost soul wandering in the desert, parched with thirst, and he was that long, cool, refreshing and lifesaving drink of water. I would never again feel like I was dying of emotional and spiritual dehydration, as long as he was there for me.

Jim knew that there was no possibility of me shedding

all of my demons and that it would take decades to distance myself from my childhood. I simply had no traditional sense of family—so he was my family, my refuge, my mentor, the father and mother I never had. I got to be the child I never really was because for the first time in my life, it was finally safe to be myself. Years of having always been on the lookout for my father had left me full of tension, apprehension, and the need to hide my real emotions. But Jim saw me for who I was, and could and should be, and he helped me to grow up with his unconditional love and support.

Hearing so many cruel stories about my childhood broke Jim's heart, so it's all the more extraordinary that when my father died in 1993 Jim encouraged me to build a bridge and try to forge an uneasy peace with my mother. I hadn't been home for more than twenty-five years!

I went to my father's funeral and found that she'd become the old woman she'd feared, ninety-three years old, grieving for her husband of nearly sixty years, tiny and frail. I began to work toward reconciliation. It wasn't easy. I still felt like a fugitive well into middle age.

My mother and I only had about a year and a half to make amends and rebuild our relationship before she had a near-fatal heart attack and massive stroke. As my mother lay dying, well beyond the point where she was capable of communicating, Jim spent countless hours holding her hand, reading to her, talking to her.

"Why are you doing this?" I asked him.

"She has a lot to teach me," he said.

I so appreciated his generosity, especially because my career in television had just started with a gig on QVC, and I was always working, working, working. This television opportunity was a godsend, as I was enmeshed in a bitter lawsuit to reclaim the use of my name, and I hadn't been allowed to work while it grinded on in the courts. Finally, a solution: television retail.

I had television obligations in Florida. My comatose mom was in Northern Maine. I never seemed to have as much time to spend with her as I wanted. She liked Jim and likely drew a great deal of comfort from him, even though she was beyond communicating directly with him. Still, I didn't quite understand Jim's cryptic remark about what he had to learn from her. I didn't know what Jim didn't yet want to tell me.

I'd had trouble feeling safe in New York since I'd been attacked, and a few years earlier, in the spring of 1989, Jim and I had moved to an old Shaker farmhouse near Danbury, Connecticut. It was peaceful and beautiful, but—located on top of a mountain on seventeen acres of land bordering the Appalachian Trail—it was also isolated.

The winter that my mom was sick, in 1994, we had a terrible blizzard. I was driving our 4x4 and managed to make it home before the worst of the storm hit. They were predicting as much as four feet of snow. I was worried about Jim, who was in our little sports car. The phone kept ringing, and each time, I hoped it would be Jim, telling me he was safe. But every time I picked it up, it was a fax tone. Finally, I turned on the fax and a message came through. It was from a hospital in Danbury, and it said: *Jim Rush. Diagnosis: Terminal Cancer.*

Shock does not even begin to describe how I felt. I knew Jim had been sick, and getting sicker as I'd heard him sometimes cry out in pain and had noticed him become melancholy and disengaged, but he had refused to discuss it with me. Anytime I brought up my suspicions with his friends, they refused to see it. Everyone was really good at denial, most of all, me. Now I knew why.

The storm raged on for hours. I stood there with the

piece of paper in my hand. Finally, Jim came home. As he walked through the door, I handed it to him.

"Do you want to talk about this?" I asked, and in that moment the roles reversed. I became the adult, and he became my child.

Jim had told his doctors not to fax him. He didn't want to have to tell me he had cancer right at the start of my television career, and when I had just weathered my long, drawn-out lawsuit. This was the crowning blow. He couldn't bear to deliver it. He knew what this would do to me.

Also, he didn't want to be treated like he was already dead, or pitied as a sick person. He wanted to go on being productive and vibrant, and live as normally as possible. I get it now. At sixty-seven, I feel the same way. The worst thing that could happen to me would be for me to be treated as infirm, or like I'm no longer useful, or I'm gone already.

Jim had secretly been getting treatment from the small-town hospital in Danbury. I insisted we move back to Manhattan so he could get top-notch care at Sloan-Kettering. He needed surgery right away, and within two months, we had closed up the farmhouse and were back in the city again.

It honestly never occurred to me that Jim would die. I

simply refused to believe it. I had developed a fairly extreme capacity for denial in order to survive my childhood, and I employed it now. I assumed that there would be a miracle. But the cancer was always a step ahead—just relentless, and it ate him alive.

A year and a half after my mother died, it became clear that Jim's final days were imminent. He wanted to make his exit his way, with dignity, and in Virginia Beach, which was his favorite place in the world. I took him down there, and we stayed in a quaint bed and breakfast—another of his favorites. I had television appearances, and Jim made me promise that I would never miss a single show. In his usual, selfless fashion, he never wanted to be a burden.

I was away in New York, about to do shows, when I got a call that Jim had been admitted into the ICU. I was told to wait until they "cleaned him up," but I went to him as soon as they let me.

I was actually so distraught when I first saw Jim, because it was clear how little time he had left, that I became hysterical and collapsed—the doctors wanted to hospitalize me as well, but I refused. I knew that I had so few remaining moments with him.

We took Jim back to the B and B. In the elevator on the way up to our room, he had a heart attack—utterly terrifying. I really understood the five stages of grief, especially the bargaining part. I offered up healthy years of my life for him to enjoy more time on earth. I pleaded with God. But of course it didn't work that way. The end had come. Jim died in my arms at dawn in the fall of 1997.

As Jim had made me promise I would, I got up from his deathbed and flew to Tampa to do a huge series of shows. Of course, HSN, where I was now appearing, would have let me out of my commitments, given what had just happened. But I had made a vow to Jim. At midnight that night, I went on the air live. I said a memorial to Jim—I'm not sure how I got through it—and I did my shows.

I didn't want to sit at home alone and cry anyhow. I wanted to be with the only family I had left, the tens of thousands of women with whom I connected through the television camera. As long as I'm in front of a TV camera lens, I never feel alone. And now that Jim was gone, this family was more important to me than ever.

I recognized even then—despite the numbing effect of my grief—what an amazing privilege it was to care for him and walk him through that door to the other side—to help him pass over peacefully. I felt truly blessed, and the experience forever changed me—taught me compassion, patience, commitment, and perhaps most of all, it taught me how precious and finite this physical life is. Not a day goes by that I don't thank the universe for my life and my health.

THE LOST DECADE

When I walked through the door of our home after the memorial service for this man who'd opened my heart, shared my struggles, lifted me spiritually, and lightened my burdens for almost twenty years, the silence was crushing. Jim was my lover and best friend, a trusted touchstone I went to daily for feedback on all things personal and professional. He was my champion and defender, my foundation, my rock. Without him I was totally overwhelmed.

"How in the hell am I going to do this thing called life without you?" I asked aloud.

Deafening silence was the only answer.

Jim had kept me grounded; now I was adrift. So much of the decade that followed was about grief and loss that I actually refer to it as "The Lost Decade."

During the years preceding his death, I'd spent the lion's share of my time and energy caring for Jim through his long, valiant struggle with cancer. I'd also been waging a legal battle against a powerful Hong Kong conglomerate that had "bought" my name a few years prior. I'd brought washable silk to the United States and achieved one of the biggest hits of my career at the time. The company had promised to develop my name into an international brand, go public on the Hang Seng index—the Hong Kong stock exchange— and make me a millionaire, but they'd failed to pay me. I'll spare you the grinding details. The upshot was a deluge of devastating legal costs and vitriol. During the battle, they'd been able to strip me of the right to use my own name, leaving me effectively blackballed from my industry and livelihood. These were truly my nightmare years, and then right after that, I endured my "lost decade."

In the midst of all this, however, serendipity had smiled on me once again, when I'd least expected it. In 1995, out of nowhere, QVC had called, asking if I would like to try designing a collection for them and appearing to sell it on their television network! I'd had to tell them that I couldn't go on-air or put a label in even a single garment using my full name. Miracle of miracles, they'd said, "No problem, we'll just introduce you as Diane!"

Careerwise, things had begun to look up. But it had been just as I was settling into becoming a regular on television—

first on QVC and then on HSN—and just as the lawsuit was finally resolving itself, as well, that Jim had passed on.

With no family, no laurels from the decades of success I'd achieved in fashion—and drained of my life savings, which I'd been forced to spend on legal fees—I turned to the only comfort I could find: food. I was used to companionship in the evenings, the pleasure of a shared meal and conversation with Jim. Without him, food became my companion, my lover, my best friend. I like to say that I became a pastagenarian, stuffing myself with heaping portions of carbohydrates each night as a solace and an escape—looking back now, I understand why we call it comfort food.

I found myself facing my fifties, alone and shattered. I was emotionally charred and physically exhausted. It felt like someone had taken a blowtorch to my soul. I barely recognized myself in the mirror. I was too numb to focus on the small details of daily life, but all the big life questions loomed, like:

> *Who am I?*
> *Without a man, can I still feel like a woman?*
> *Without money, can I still feel blessed?*
> *Without clout, can I still feel powerful?*

I know now that the answer to all of the above is *Hell yes!* But as I trudged into my mid-fifties, freshly bereaved and now sixty pounds overweight, fear, doubt, and self-judgment prevailed. My personal life was a numb silence.

I was grateful for my television career, but as a designer, I was simply cranking out the type of clothes that my kind and I were expected to wear: appropriately nondescript "mid-life" garb—baggy pants and oversized camp shirts— that said *hide me*, instead of vibrant fashion that said *see me*. I was good at it, and it provided a living, which I very much needed, but it was hardly my dream.

The one positive thing I can say about this time in my life is that I was still basking in one of the most hard-earned, but important, lessons of my life: a lesson in gratitude. I'd learned it while I was caring for Jim during his brutal battle against cancer. In the final stage of his illness, and the days surrounding his death, no matter the numbing effect of the grief and loss I was feeling, I was very aware of what an enormous privilege it was to be there to help and support him. This was partly because he was such an amazing person, who continued to teach me invaluable and universal truths during every moment we had together, no matter how sick he was. And also because dealing up close and personal with the most primal aspects of the human experience—life and death—is profoundly altering.

Toward the end of Jim's illness, I was so strung out from physical and emotional exhaustion, and so burnt out by his suffering and the unfairness of it all that I wasn't sure I wanted to go on without him—I wasn't sure I wanted to be in a world without Jim, my protector, my guide, my father, my mother, my brother, my everything.

We both held a deep belief in reincarnation and felt we had lived many past lives together, and this was a major component of our shared spirituality and overall closeness. And it seemed like it would be so much better if we could both just start again together, enter a new lifetime that was fresh and free of pain.

I was by Jim's bed one day when I confessed to him how I was feeling. "I don't want to go on in a world without you," I said.

I will never forget his response: "Diane, we've lived lifetimes together, some as warriors on the battlefield," he said. "Surely at some point, as we fought side by side, you were mortally wounded, and I had to carry you back to a cave, or behind a huge boulder, and lay you down and comfort you as best I could, and then leave you to go back out to the battle and carry on the fight. That's what you've got to do with me right now. You can't save me. And you have to go on and achieve everything we've built and fought for together. Please promise me you will never give up."

Of course I made this promise to him. He was dying. How could I not? But it wasn't just something I said to comfort him. I promised from my heart, and I've kept this promise ever since, even on the darkest days and longest nights without him. I have never given up, and I never will.

When it was time for Jim to pass over peacefully, with as much dignity as possible, he died in my arms at dawn. In that moment, it was as if a door opened, and he walked into a great white light. In my mind's eye, I visualized it so clearly. That intense light bathed me—just for an instant, but in that amazing moment, it infused me with what I can only describe as an elevated experience, a blessed feeling, one that lasted for several years and had me operating at a refined, higher vibration, a heightened level of consciousness. It was like being touched by an angel. I truly believe this was Jim's parting gift to me.

No matter what was happening in my day-to-day life during those first years after Jim passed—and as I've just expressed, much of it was very rough, truth be told—I didn't get petty or angry or jealous or quibble over the trivial. To put it simply, I cruised along, above it all—still deeply enmeshed in my grief—but no longer sweating the small stuff.

I can remember so vividly being in the television studio right after Jim died and having someone bitch at me about my feet, and how they were going to look in the shoes I was supposed to be wearing in that segment. I thought to myself: *Someone just died in my arms—do you really think this is a big deal, something to lose it over? Is this how you want to use your energy?* It was as if my energetic vibration had been sped up a thousandfold, and cleaned me of any negativity, like I was cruising along beyond the speed of sound, so that all of the petty blah-blah was silenced, and none of the normal idle chatter and gossip of daily life could penetrate me.

Every time I felt lost, which was every other minute, and I was wondering why Jim wasn't there with me because I felt like I needed an answer that could come only from him, I heard his voice in my head, during a conversation we'd had in the days before he passed. He said, "You and I have had tens of thousands of hours of conversation. You already have all the answers. I'm gonna die, but those conversations are distilled in your memory. Every time you need me, I'll be there. Just reach into your memory bank." To this day, I live by the tenets he taught me, and I find it profoundly comforting to know that he is still inside of me, and beside me, because that's where I've finally realized that all of the answers are—inside of *me*.

I always wondered when Jim was going to come to me after he passed, and I kept waiting for it to happen. About eight months went by before I finally had a vivid, unnerving dream about him. I dreamed I was in one of New York City's iconic buildings—the Chrysler Building, maybe—at rush hour. I stepped off an elevator into the lobby and looked outside into the street, and there were people everywhere—thousands of them.

In the distance in front of me, I saw Jim, his healthy, pre-cancer self, the one I had known and loved for years before he became sick. I somehow knew, even in my dream, that he was dead, but there he was! I couldn't believe it! I was so excited. I went running after him across the lobby, trying to catch up to him.

I found myself out on the street among thousands of people who were scurrying to and fro, hurrying home from work when suddenly I realized that, although I was dressed in business attire, I was barefoot (strange!), and the sidewalk was paved in broken glass! I looked down at my feet, which were already being cut by the glass, and asked myself: *Do I love him enough to run after him, even if it means tearing my feet to shreds running over this broken glass, even if I only get to have one last minute of conversation with him?* Of course the answer was *yes*!

I ran after him, and although he looked back at me once, I never did catch up to him as he descended into the subway and disappeared. I had lost him. It was so painful to see him go, and yet it was also a reminder of the great gift of love and deep, eternal connection that we had shared, and how that continued to live on inside of me.

I think this is particularly important for us to remember as we age and lose people who have been essential to our lives—parents, siblings, spouses, lovers, and friends. Everywhere we've been, everyone we've loved, every moment of life has had a profound effect in shaping who we are right now. And we have the ability to access all of those hearts and minds, all of those places and moments, all of the time.

As hard as it was to lose Jim, the tragedy became a profound gift, and ever since, I've always felt that the heightened experience I gained in the aftermath of his passing is exactly what aging should be like: the ability to achieve an intense focus on the aspects of life that really matter while the trivial falls away.

It was from this energetic place that I eventually rediscovered myself and achieved the greatest success and happiness of my life. I've always believed this energy gift, and all that it brought me, was Jim's blessing for me to go on living.

Immediately after Jim's passing, even though I was so distraught and worn out, at that moment when his spirit left his body, when the light bathed me, I felt I was composed of a million points of light—points of shimmering energy— that I was a sparkling being. It soon became clear that the sum of experiences had changed me forever, taught me the greatest compassion, patience, commitment, and most of all, how infinitely precious this physical life is, every minute and every second of it.

Because of this incredible experience, one of the great pluses of growing older for me is my sense of appreciation.

Every precious moment seems so much more piquant now than it ever did before. There's a sense of urgency—but one that's sweet, not unrelenting—to not only get things done, but to also set my sights on accomplishing more.

Before I could fully appreciate all of this, though, I still had my "lost decade" to overcome, which I'm about to go into in detail in the First Simple Truth. Somewhere along the way between youth and middle age, I'd utterly lost myself. But the Sixties call to individuality I'd grown up with still resonated within me. I still had the courage I'd had when my friends and I invaded L.A. thrift stores and paraded ourselves down Sunset Boulevard in vintage raccoon coats, Victorian petticoats, cowboy boots, and amazing jeans.

I could still remember vividly how, when I'd heard Bob Dylan sing "Forever Young" at the last concert for The Band—captured in Martin Scorsese's incredible 1978 film, *The Last Waltz*—the lyrics had touched me so deeply that I cried. Even in my youth, I'd known that I wanted to age in an eternal way, an ageless way. I'd believed (maybe naively, but deeply) that I could, and should, age into someone more beautiful, more vibrant, more powerful, and more precious than any younger woman could be—that the accumulating years should amount to something.

"Age is a question of mind over matter," said legendary baseball pitcher Satchel Paige. "If you don't mind, it doesn't matter."

It could have been that simple, but I'd lost the thread of who I was and what my own unique life path was supposed to be. Then, as sixty loomed, I got a wake-up call, which I'll get to in the next chapter. It forced me to take a long, hard look at my life. I was still alive. I didn't know if I'd ever find another truly great love, but I wasn't ready to quit on the opposite sex—or on my own sexuality either. I wasn't ready to quit on myself or my dreams.

Slowly, over time, I excavated myself from that cocoon of fat and grieving—both for my life partner and my youth. She was still in there—that bangin' rocker chick—under the rubble of heartbreak and life's hard knocks. All the water under the bridge of my life hadn't diluted the essence of me, that girl in the hot jeans. Someone once said to me, "As a woman, it's dangerous to grow old," which caused me to think to myself, *Bloody hell, it's even more dangerous not to!*

So with sixty fast approaching, I made a conscious decision to take a radically proactive approach to aging: *If it's going to happen, I'm going to do it right. I'm going to do it on my terms.*

With no guidelines to follow and no icons to emulate, I set out to recover my joy, reinvent my body, rebuild my fashion empire, and open my heart to the possibility that I might find another full-on, romance novel–caliber love. From the ashes of grief and financial ruin, I was determined to rise like a phoenix and create a spiritually, sexually, and professionally rewarding Act III for this extraordinary life I had fought so hard to take back from my parents and shape into my own dream.

Early in 2012, simply by chance, I read a magazine excerpt that really summed it up for me. In the section I encountered of Kati Maron's memoir about bereavement and resilience, *Paris: A Love Story*, she writes: "I have never wanted to hold my life tighter, or to live more fully than now, reeling from loss. So. My life must be reinvented. No living backward. No living forward. Living in the present."

I realized that's exactly what I'd done after my "lost decade" and what I would continue to do for the rest of my life. I recommitted myself to the mission at the heart of this book, which became clear for me as I sat down to write:

We must have the courage to perpetually reinvent ourselves, and we must have the wisdom to always live in the now.

Along the way, since my "lost decade" and in the writing of this book, I developed the principles that guide me now. A few struck like bolts from out of the blue; some had to sink in over time. But when added up, they answer the question that I am asked quite often, and often ask myself: "How in the world do you do it?"

These are my Ten Simple Truths.

PART II:

TEN
SIMPLE
TRUTHS

THE FIRST SIMPLE TRUTH:

IT'S REALLY NOT THAT COMPLICATED.

(So, don't overthink it!)

We tend to make the aging process complex with our denial, fear, and psychological clutter, but every once in a while—if we're lucky—someone throws a bucket of cold water on us, and we're forced to wake up to a crystal-clear reality in which using our usual excuses and turning a blind eye just don't cut it anymore.

❧ A REAL EYE-OPENER ❧

After Jim died, I avoided visiting my primary care physician for years. I'd seen my share of clinics, hospitals, and waiting rooms while Jim was sick, and I didn't want anything more to do with the medical community. Or at least that's what I told myself. I think, deep down, I knew that I was in serious denial about the state of my health, but I was absolutely not ready or able to see it yet.

I kept my nose to the grindstone and ignored the repeated reminders my body gave me that I was long overdue for the standard lube, oil, and tune-up. At nearly sixty years old, and now sixty pounds overweight, these were some serious reminders: constant aches and pains in my back and knees, shortness of breath, frequent depression, and a total lack of energy and libido.

I managed to avoid my doctor for more than three years, but he badgered me endlessly and finally threatened to drop me as a patient. I caved and scheduled a checkup.

As I sat in the examination room, I squirmed uncomfortably on a plastic chair, finding it hard to breath. I was nervous, and to be totally honest, the rolls of fat on my stomach were constricting my diaphragm.

When my doctor walked into the room, his head snapped back. He actually reeled slightly, not even attempting to disguise how startled he was at my appearance.

The first thing he said after greeting me was, "Why don't you get on the scale and let me weigh you?"

"No, thanks," I said. "I'm really not in the mood for that."

"Let's do it anyway," he said.

"Okay," I sighed, "but I'm going to keep my eyes closed."

As I stepped onto the scale, I heard it tip. I heard him slide the indicator up a notch to the next fifty pounds. And then, he pried my eyes open, gently but firmly parting the lids with his thumb and index finger until I had no choice but to see what was in front of me.

"Take a look, Diane. You are a quarter of a pound away from the clinical definition of obesity for your height."

I weighed 179¾ pounds.

"Oh, my God . . . ," I whispered.

"You need to do something about this," he said.

It's not like I hadn't noticed I was gaining weight. I'd been rail thin by the time Jim died. Between the fact that he was unable to eat and the emotional stress I was under, I hadn't been able to eat much, either. But then I'd been left alone with my sorrow, and comfort food was—well, it really was comforting! Settling into an easy chair with a giant bowl of pasta was better than crawling into bed and pulling the blankets over my head, because bed is kind of a sad place when you've just lost the love of your life.

A hectic work schedule and constant travel hadn't helped, either. By the time I stood on the scale in that doctor's office, roughly six years after Jim died, I'd packed on about sixty pounds. So he certainly wasn't cluing me into something I didn't already know, but to hear him put it in those words— "clinical obesity"—was a kick in the head.

The people who cared about me had been too sympathetic to say anything. Or maybe too afraid. (I can be a bit intense.)

Either way, no one came right out and said, "Geez, Diane, you're really getting fat." Thank God this doctor was kind enough to be cruel; he put into words what I had been denying for years; what no one else had the courage to say to me; what I hadn't had the courage to say to myself.

I was fat. Borderline obese!

I had eaten my way through grief, loss, frustration, and loneliness. Now the secret was out. I was fat, and I hated it, and hated myself for it. In one of the most vivid moments of my life, my doctor had literally opened my eyes. Not only did he tell me the brutal truth, but he also told me I had to change. When he laid that mandate on me, he didn't leave any room for doubt. He didn't say, "You should think about," or, "You might try." No—he said, "You need to do something, and you need to do it now!"

Again, not telling me anything I didn't already know. But in the moment, as his words sank in, the reality of what I was going to have to do felt like facing Mount Everest.

I responded numbly to the rest of the exam, and as I exited his office onto Central Park South, I burst into tears. Crossing the street quickly, I descended into Central Park and walked for a while, finally sitting by a pond to reflect, tears streaming down my face.

I thought about how unhappy the past few years had been and how profoundly it had affected my health, my self-esteem, my social life, my ability to function as a fashion figure. The weight gain was just the tip of the iceberg. Closing in on sixty, I felt all the apprehension women in our culture are programmed to feel about aging, plus all the magnified age-phobia that comes with having been in the youth-obsessed fashion industry my whole life.

Sixty?

Six decades?

This was a big one. Totally uncharted territory.

According to everything I'd seen and learned, sixty spelled old age and everything that came with that—none of it welcome. None of it positive. So many of my dreams were unfulfilled, and at my age, they were likely to stay that way. My body was racked with aches and pains. When I looked in the mirror—and believe me, I didn't to do it frequently—I saw a stranger. My family is known for it's longevity; we all live into our high nineties, but frankly, the thought of spending forty more years on a slow but steep downhill decline wasn't exactly appealing.

Does it really have to be this way? I wondered.

On a purely functional level—all fear and denial aside—I asked myself: *Am I actually helpless, or can I work with the process? Can I pick and choose my battles and negotiate aging? Can I actually make aging an advantage, make every passing year a plus, and recapture the joy, the confidence, the love of life that came so naturally to me in my youth?*

The answer was, *Hell yes!*

As soon as I heard that rallying cry crescendo within myself, there was room for only one thought: *I have to do this.*

I wanted this. I needed this.

But immediately, questions crowded in: *How do I do this?*

And then it struck me. There was only one way forward: *Just do it!*

 THE LIST

Being the pragmatic career girl I am, everything for me

begins with a list: a list of what I'm packing to fly to London, a list of weekend chores when I'm home, a list of design goals for the week ahead.

Forming the List as a way to assess my life as it was and my path to something better seemed natural. Sitting beside the pond on that crisp spring afternoon, I pulled a crumpled piece of paper and a pen from my bag. I drew lines, creating three columns and a bar across the top, and began charting a tangible, truthful, very personal inventory.

In the first column, I listed everything that I liked about my life and myself. In other words, the short list. This didn't take long.

LIKE
[1] Designing clothing
[2] Being on television
[3] Living in NYC
[4] Frequent travel
[5] Being my own boss

In the second column, I listed everything that I didn't like about my life and myself—the long list—starting with my obvious weight problem. This was a manifestation of a lot of issues—physical, emotional, and social—but it was a symptom, not the cause, of my unhappiness and general sense of being uncomfortable in my own, now middle aged body.

DISLIKE

[1] Serious weight gain

[2] No social life—lonely!

[3] No dating or male companionship

[4] Aching joints, bad back pain, poor digestion

[5] Hugely reduced sex drive

[6] Feel marginalized in the mainstream culture, like the "Invisible Woman"

[7] Can't fit into any cool clothes anymore

[8] Treated as if irrelevant, like an old lady

[9] Look much older on the outside than I really am inside

[10] No sex life

In the third column, I listed realistic steps I could take to restore my emotional and physical health, and regain my balance. I kept the List simple, and as I put it all down on paper in black and white, I saw it really wasn't all that complicated. It was easy to identify where change could be effected immediately (even though the results might take awhile), what I could handle on my own, and where I might need professional help.

For example, in the "Dislike" column, "Serious weight gain," was at the top of my List. Writing it down, I could truly admit it to myself. Moving on to the "What I Can Do About It" column forced me to ask myself, "Why?" Instead of focusing on the symptom, I had to get to the root cause—what did eating mean to me? What did eating do for me?

Since Jim's death, I'd sworn off men, hidden myself at home, and made food my boyfriend, my love interest, my companion, my confidant. (Note to self: Next time you need a sixty-pound companion, get an Irish setter!) I really hated being overweight, and that led to many of the other dislikes on the List: low energy, knee and back pain, health problems, loss of self-esteem, low sex drive, no more cool girl wardrobe, and so on. Identifying the cause of the weight problem made it solvable, and solving the weight problem immediately eliminated a lot of other problems on the List. Looking back, it is impossible to quantify how much I gained from taking that first step: Losing the weight!

WHAT I CAN DO ABOUT IT

[1] Weight gain—lose weight!

[2] This is the key to changing #1, #2, #3, #4, #5, #6, #7, #8, #9, #10—finding this one key problem leads to solving so many more.

Making the List was a pivotal moment in my life. Not only was it an admission, but also it simplified things by distilling the nebulous fog of dissatisfaction and discomfort—and quite frankly, depression. It brought the real issues into focus, forcing me to hone in on the cause of each problem in order to define a solution. And it paved the way forward with a clear, step-by-step action plan that was well within my power to execute. And it made me feel like I was once again in control of my runaway-freight-train life.

As I worked through the long process of losing the weight and getting myself back (I repeat: the looooooong process), The List anchored me and helped me navigate shifting circumstances, good and bad. Every time I felt confused or befuddled by life's unexpected turns and the natural, inevitable changes in and around me, I returned to the List.

I still do. I tweak it—add to it and delete from it—constantly.

Over the years, through trial and error, success and failure, triumph and tragedy, I developed my own mantra: *See. Do. Be.*

> *See*—your challenges, honestly.
> *Do*—activate what you need to do to
>   correct them.
> *Be*—the new, improved, and reinvented
>   you!

The List never fails me. It is an everyday working tool for me now, and I go back to it all of the time, even though it looks different than it did that first day. It always serves to clarify and determine a call to action, even in the most confusing of life scenarios. A challenge that seems like a tangled maze from the outside is "just a thang" when you break it down. It is what it is. Chances are you already know what needs to be done about it; you just need a little help opening your eyes, like the honest advice I was lucky enough to get from my doctor at just the right moment.

I'm not saying it was easy. It was a lot of work, and there was no roadmap to follow, no programmed personal GPS, no "here's how to assemble" instruction manual. I had only my internal compass to steer by. If I'd allowed myself to dwell on all the logistics, obstacles, blind corners, and unknowns—not to mention the opinions of the cast of characters that populate my personal and professional life—I would have been overwhelmed by the enormity and complexity of the task. If I'd depended on someone else to show up and lead me by the hand, I'd still be sitting there in Central Park, waiting for my life to somehow start over.

But I'm not. Because, with age sixty looming on the horizon, I decided I was not about to "go gently into that good night." I kept thinking of that Peggy Lee song, "Is That All There Is?" And I had a new answer: *Hell no!*

But first, to make the journey out of the dark woods of grief and shame, denial, and lethargy that I was in, I had to forgive myself. I realized that I hadn't done anything horribly wrong or irredeemable. I'd in fact done something pretty great—I'd survived and aged. Jim had stopped aging, and I knew I didn't want that.

I'd been beating myself up when the truth was that I'd simply changed—and along the way gotten a little lost—but it became clear that the me I was in the process of finding again could be even better than the me I had misplaced. I saw it was important to draw on every ounce of determination I had, because like any other rescue mission, this was going to be hard work. And it wasn't going to happen overnight.

To complete the task, you have to really love this person who needs your help—namely you!

And that brings me to an important point. I didn't show anyone the List for several years. It wasn't for them. It was for me. Believe me, I got enough unsolicited responses from people as I began overhauling and reinventing myself. The last thing I wanted was any more negativity or confusion in my life based on the misconceptions my friends might have about my List. I was embarrassed enough by the items it contained.

You shouldn't feel like you have to show anyone your list, either. In fact, you'll have a much easier time being honest with yourself and sticking to it if you don't. And why should you, anyhow? Quite frankly, this is between you and you. And it's no one's business but your own.

You have every right—at any age—to be happy, healthy,

sexually active, uplifted, and fulfilled for as long as you draw breath. Chances are, people in your life might doubt your mission, but they won't argue with the results. But until those results start materializing—and they will!—the last thing you need is a Greek chorus on the sidelines, telling you that your undertaking is impossible or irrelevant, when it's anything but.

That said, if you have a partner who's open and supportive and willing, you can absolutely do this together. It could be great for your relationship—a joint mission, a shared raison d'être. Many of the aspects of aging that you're not happy about will probably be the same as your partner's, and acknowledging them and making a plan for change together can be invigorating—even fun—and downright sexy.

On the other hand, some partners will be threatened by your decision to suddenly lose forty pounds and get your life back on track. That's okay. This isn't about them. It's about you. And if I've learned one thing over the years, it's to keep my own counsel and not to ask for permission for anything from anyone. As I realized from the toxic environment in which my parents raised me, just because everyone around you says no doesn't mean that what you want to do is wrong.

It just means the people around you don't want you to do it, for their own personal reasons.

Change is never easy. But the fact is that change happens naturally, for better or worse. The real issue is how you deal with it. See it as a good thing! Celebrate it. Work with it. Steer it. Manage it, even.

Samuel Ullman wrote, "You are as young as your faith, as old as your doubt; as young as your self-confidence, as old as your fear; as young as your hope, as old as your despair."

Don't let the inevitability of change make you its fearful slave. You have the power to shape change in your favor. I admit, it's not a cakewalk. But what's so great about easy anyhow? Easy is how I gained sixty pounds. And hard work can actually be a good thing—it gives you a focus, a purpose, a sense of control.

Maybe up until now, the meaning in your life has been rooted in your children, and you're facing an empty nest for the first time. After decades of putting others first, the moment has come for you to do for yourself.

Maybe you've always been a career woman, but now you're winding down or even heading toward retirement. Again, put your focus on yourself, take the challenge, reinvent yourself. Maybe it's time to develop a hidden or dormant talent, or build a second career from a longtime love, like cooking, or decorating, or whatever you've daydreamed about doing for years.

See. Do. Be.

❧ SO LET'S GET STARTED! ☙

OK, baby boomer sisters and brothers, just in case your primary care physician isn't as brutally honest as mine was, I'm about to grab you by the eyelids. I'm challenging you to open your eyes and conduct a truthful, thorough inventory of your life. See it as a call to arms!

It's time for you to make a List for yourself. Set aside some private time, pour that glass of wine or cup of tea, turn on the stereo, curl up on the sofa—set the mood—but settle down and do it!

The most important thing is to take a complete—and completely honest—self-inventory.

There's no other way forward—and forward is definitely the direction we all want to go.

And, as I've said, I'll bet you know the truth deep down inside of you anyhow. I did. The real truth. Not the dowdy, overweight, sexless woman I had accidentally become. But the bodacious, bangin' career maven and sexual goddess that I was meant to be all along.

The essential me was a lean, cocky, naturally sexy, smart Jewish girl who was hyper-fashionable, a cool dresser, a trendsetter, a New York *Sex and the City* babe. I had lost so much of her, but she was still lurking in there somewhere. If not, how else would I have found her inside of me when I called her out of hiding and rescued her from being held hostage by all of that extra girth?

Your list is going to look different than mine. Don't worry—that means you did it right. But I'll bet your list will have a lot in common with my list. And the lists of all the other women who are reading this book right now. That's why there's nothing to be ashamed of—not for how far you may have fallen from your ideal, or how much more you still want from your life but don't know how to get—because it's universal. Primal. Human. And regaining it is so within your reach! I promise you that.

Once you've made your list, you'll probably wonder,

Where the hell do I begin? I know I did. Which brings me to the most important part of the process, because it's the first step after you've made your list, which makes it the one from which all of your success emanates. You've mustered your courage and decided change is necessary. You've gotten honest about what needs to change.

Now, see.

Pick *one* item on the list of things that you don't like about your life or about your aging self that you can absolutely do something about *right now.* Start there. For the time being, forget about the rest of The List.

For me, that *one* central issue, which was also the first problem to address, was my weight. All I focused on for the first year after I made The List was getting my weight under control. And I did—slowly but surely, pound by pound.

This goal wasn't easy. Obviously, I knew a thing or two about denial, given that I'd let myself gain sixty pounds as a defensive wall of fat between me and the world, not only without acknowledging it—but also by perpetrating a whole elaborate set of self-denial and lies about how it didn't matter, and how I didn't care, and how it was all an inevitable part of aging anyhow.

I had seen my business partner walk by my office, seen his eyes pop as he registered the fat visibly rolling over my waistline and shook his head in disgust and dismay; seen him worry how I was going to stay viable as a television personality, a role on which our business depended, with the way I looked; intuited his internal debate over whether he was going to have to confront me or not. After all, we were talking about our livelihoods, here!

I had noticed that men no longer flirted with me and—even more than that—had noticed that they didn't even make eye contact or look at me anymore.

So the antidote to all of these issues, both in my professional and private life, was losing the weight. It was difficult to revamp my eating habits, but it was manageable. If I had tried to tackle everything on that list all at once, I would have gotten overwhelmed and discouraged, and quit!

But getting up every morning with one mantra in my mind—*lose the weight*—was simple enough to keep me on track. And with each pound shed, I felt more empowered, more in control, more sure of myself.

I tackled the next two parts of the plan: *do* and *be.* I took action. I cut calories. I shifted from carbs to protein. I exer-

cised. I embodied my goal. I felt purposeful. I felt powerful.
I felt increasingly successful. I lost the weight.

Everything else got easier. Like magic—but over time—
a bunch of other problems on the List disappeared. My aches
and pains diminished, and finally vanished. My energy
slowly returned. I began to feel more comfortable in my own
skin, and as I did, I came out of the cocoon of my grief more
and more, like a little baby chick, pecking and clawing its
way out of its shell toward the light and freedom—I no
longer felt like a prisoner of my own flesh.

I was triumphant! I had value. I began to feel more and
more confident. My self-esteem returned. I was getting my
groove back. I had achieved something consequential. I
could do more, and maybe more importantly, now I wanted
to do more. My call out to the universe was *bring it on!*

I tackled additional items on the List. As I did, change
actually got easier. Nothing was as hard as that first step had
been. In the same way that a healthy metabolism will speed
up with more activity, it was as if the metabolism of my
life had sped up, and the positive energy of my initial change
was fueling and driving all of the other changes that I wanted
and desperately needed to make. Not only did it get easier,

but also, the results got exponentially better—as if the new "whole me" was so much greater than the previously fragmented parts had been.

It took me a long time, but I finally talked to my (male) doctor about my fading libido—again, it wasn't easy to "go public" with such a private, hyperpersonal topic. I also did research and found herbal and dietary remedies. I looked good; I felt good; I was ready to share myself with someone. Well, sort of ready . . . it had been a while! (To be honest . . . a long while!)

As they say, all work and no play is no way to live, even when, like me, your work is play.

If you're willing to be truly honest, brave, and proactive, you can repurpose your life and be much more comfortable in your skin—and maybe even happier—than you've ever been before. Just take it from me. If anyone had told me at thirty, or forty, or fifty that my sixties would be the most focused, productive, enjoyable, successful, meaningful, and precious years of my life, I would have said that's insane. But it's not. It's true. And if I can do it, anybody can do it! It can be your truth, too! Make your List. You have nothing to lose and everything to gain! *See! Do! Be!*

THE SECOND SIMPLE TRUTH:

THE CLASSIC RULEBOOK IS OBSOLETE.

(Toss it!)

Okay, hang on to that List you just made. We're going to revisit it at the end of this chapter and tweak it with the important understanding that a lot of the dos and don'ts, shoulds and shouldn'ts—just about everything you've been fed your whole life about how "older women" are supposed to look, think, and behave, when we're supposed to peak, when we're expendable, and what our role is supposed to be after our childbearing years—are about to go out the window. After all, if I hadn't thrown out that rulebook, so to speak, I would never have designed my first jeans and started a revolution!

The classic rulebook for women—the unwritten but unmistakable guidelines applied to "women of a certain age"—is part myth, part antiquated ideal, and part outmoded judgment.

> *Act your age.* (**Whatever that means.**)
> *No sex after sixty.*
> *Don't show your arms. Don't show your legs.*
>   *Don't wear a bikini.* (**Just be invisible.**)
> *Wear short hair and long skirts.*

These are just some of the messages that bombard us. No wonder Shakespeare called old age "the winter of our discontent"! No wonder we women are terrified of aging!

Sure, accepting those rules for aging—or rather, being swept along by them—is the proverbial "path of least resistance" most of the time. Just give up everything that is "You"—everything that defined your female life force.

Or don't. It's really up to you. Honestly! Beyond basic right and wrong, everything else is just accessorizing.

Maybe your own path, bumpy and imperfect though it may be, is a better way for you. Of course, how to find that path may be a mystery, which is why so many of us take a while to find it or don't find it ever—getting lost, instead, in the tangled maze of aging and all of the unfamiliar twists and turns that come along with it.

Let me give you a very personal example.

KEEP YOUR JEANS ON!

Determined, I stuck to a diet and exercise program, lost sixty pounds, and made the lifestyle adjustments necessary to keep that weight off. I don't want to minimize the effort; it was a hefty undertaking (pardon the pun), and it didn't just manifest itself on the surface. I changed my attitude to save my life!

I actually had to reprogram my brain about what food meant to me. I don't want to spend a lot of time here detailing exactly how I did it. But let's just say that, again, it started with being honest with myself, and with making a List.

I wrote down what I was eating (*tons of carbs, in particular pasta, and too much of it*), when I was eating it (*at night, after the excitement and fun of my day was over*), and why (*because I was lonely, and sad, and I wanted to literally pad myself against the pain of losing someone I'd loved deeply*).

But I also did a lot of research in addition to my soul-searching. About how much the metabolism slows down after age forty. About how we really don't need that much food to function at our best. About the best times during the day to eat and still burn calories. About how if I were going to indulge in my vice—carbohydrates—I should absolutely do so before three p.m., so that my body would have time to burn them off during the rest of the day.

Based on what I learned—about both myself and nutrition—I made a personalized plan. I exercised vigorously for an hour each morning. I ate one big meal a day, centered around vegetables and a healthy high-grade protein that wasn't red meat, at noon. When I wasn't socializing in the evening, I didn't eat after three p.m., except for a light snack and herbal tea. And I cut out most alcohol—no more high-calorie margaritas—just an occasional white wine.

During the process of implementing my plan, I figured out, through trial and error, what worked for me and what I was capable of doing. It didn't take long for me to feel better. I realized I had been tired all of the time, not only because I was carrying so much weight around, but also because I had been overburdening my body with too much of the wrong foods.

Eating light and healthy, I suddenly had a lot more energy, which made it easier to stay active, and in turn, continue to keep my weight down. Not only had I changed, but also I found that I liked life under the new regime much better. I finally felt like I was steering my own ship again.

My discipline obviously comes in part from seeing myself on television. There's nowhere to hide when you're in front of the camera. But, don't fool yourself, there's really nowhere to hide inside of ourselves, either.

If weight loss and reshaping your body are among the top issues on your version of the List, you'll have to be very frank with yourself and maybe give up some foods you love and habits that have become ingrained over the years. But, trust me, it will be *so* worth it! And fun—really! Think of losing as winning—and winning is fun!

Like I did, begin with one goal and strive for a results-driven solution. As a part of my focus on weight loss, I made exercise a goal-oriented, solution-driven game. I chose a part of my body—first, my chubby, mushy, flapping-in-the-breeze, out-of-shape upper arms, which I have been ashamed of my entire life. I exercised those triceps and biceps furiously, and then, I smiled furiously from ear to ear the first time I saw the muscles in my arms ripple. Once again, I felt the power of focus and the results that can be achieved with it. And then, for the first time in my life, at age sixty-two, I started proudly wearing sleeveless dresses and (once again) felt very in control and very "cool girl." Maybe my approach will be useful for you; pick one body part that really bugs you and start there.

My mantra for dieting and exercise is twenty pounds off = twenty years younger!! Weight gain is a major ager.

Losing the weight and reshaping my body was just part of the process, but as I worked to resolve that top-priority issue on my List, a lot of other smaller issues fell into place, including the major important of being able to wear fashion again, to look and feel a bit like "me" again, to emote just a bit of sex appeal, and to be able to wear the ultimate "cool girl" accessory again—slammin' jeans! For me, being able to don denim again was more than a dream or a goal; it was a necessity.

Back in the day, jeans were my native language, my favorite form of self-expression, and my entrée to the glamorous life of beautiful people, music legends, and free-spirited artists. As I shed layer after layer of fat and inertia and depression, I discovered that the bangin' rocker chick was still alive and well, just buried under layers of fat, only slightly altered and waiting to be rescued from the rubble of denial that had accumulated with the passing years. All the water under the bridge of my life hadn't done a thing to change the essence of me: that long-legged girl in the hot jeans.

Conventional wisdom (that rusty old rulebook) decreed that a woman my age shouldn't even think about wearing sexy jeans. I disagreed. My first conscious act of aging agelessly was the determination to bring jeans back into my life.

Unfortunately—or fortunately for me, in the long run—there weren't any out there. Finding jeans that fit the new me (or the old me—or more honestly—the middle aged me) was almost impossible.

Frustrated with what was available (and not), I did the same thing I'd done when I was a teenager and couldn't find jeans that fit my individual style: I created them. I envisioned a line of jeans that would fit a woman's body instead of expecting her body to fit the jeans.

Everyone in fashion told me, "You are crazy. You're wasting your time. Your target audience won't wear jeans. They can't wear jeans. Besides, no one wants to see 'old fat chicks' in jeans."

There's that obsolete rulebook again!

In the fashion industry, youth is an obsession, and skinny is everything. Their philosophy says: Hook the customer at fourteen, keep her addicted to your brand 'til she hits thirty-five, then forget about her unless she's ageing like Jennifer Lopez! Jeans, they all reasoned, should be marketed to twenty-somethings by a young pop star—or in the tele-retailing world where I was selling my designs, a young soap opera star with a microscopic one-inch butt!

The me who had been crushed by Jim's death and the

exhausting grind of my legal battle to regain the right to use my name might have stopped right there. But having shed the weight I'd been hiding behind for so long, I'd uncovered another me that was a lot closer to the rebellious free spirit of my youth—the "strut your stuff" babe I'd been when I was creating jeans for other free-spirited women like Janis Joplin. So I didn't listen to conventional wisdom—instead, I fought back!

Now, wait a minute! There you are excluding me again! I thought. *But not if I have anything to say about it*—that universal rejection became a battle cry and a purpose-driven call to arms!

I believed in my jeans. I wanted to wear them! And I wanted to share them. The idea became a goal, and the goal became a mission. Once again, I was graced with serendipity—a new leadership team took over my television network, HSN, where I was still selling the "hide me" middle aged washable silk clothing for which I was known. The new CEO was a brilliant, glamorous fashionista—and a baby boomer who loved wearing jeans and who saw the logic of the light-bulb moment that had brought me back to jeans. So she gave me my chance.

At the time, no one in fashion was making jeans for baby boomer women. No one! To be totally honest, I'd never made jeans, myself. Yes, I'd embroidered, beaded, hand-painted, hand-dyed and customized rock stars' own personal jeans, but I'd never actually created a pair from a pattern I made myself—created all the measurements from scratch—and I certainly hadn't mass-produced them.

I wasn't exactly getting a lot of support, either.

"These measurements make no sense," I heard. My business partner and other members of my industry were less than enthusiastic. Everyone kept saying: "The waist is too big; the legs are too skinny; the front and back rise are too high."

But it all made sense to me. They reflected the way we biologically age as women. Instead of designing these jeans for a size-zero, twentysomething mannequin, I'd used myself as the fit model—my own almost-sixty-year-old body in all its imperfect glory, which even after I'd lost the weight had its ever-present "junk in the trunk." And, surprise, surprise, that "junk in the trunk" that at one point used to annoy me suddenly served me well in creating an "honest" fit for my baby boomer jeans.

The first time I put on the original sample pair, I walked down Fifth Avenue, and a guy working in a manhole whistled and yelled, "Looking good!" I hadn't heard that in eons!

That made my day. It made my week! It justified all my efforts—and it told me I was onto something big!

I hadn't worn jeans in more than a decade (because I couldn't). All that time, I'd been hiding a body that truly didn't belong to me in camouflage clothes other people thought I should wear. Now that I was back, in my true body, wearing my true skin—a pair of fabulous, shape-hugging jeans—I was deluged by a torrent of great memories. Passing by the shop windows that reflected my image, I saw fleeting reflections of all the places in my life where I'd worn jeans—all the sunny days, all the laid-back moments—which, given the fact that I'd been a part of the first ever (fashion) denim generation—was a lot. I felt like I was back in the streaming flow of humanity again. Like I had my mojo back! Though I don't normally like to see myself as part of a pack, in this one aspect of life, I really do, and I like it! Jeans are truly about belonging instead of conforming.

Women of my generation shaped like me—or shaped like themselves, whatever that may be—don't step into the fitting room and see the standard jeans as wrong. They're programmed to see themselves as wrong. Trying on jeans as a baby boomer feels more like a punishment—a push-back, a guaranteed rejection, a negative experience. But not my jeans!

Rocking my newly created jeans on Fifth Avenue, I was instantly galvanized, prepared to be a champion for those women who were being excluded from the pack, like me. Somehow I was sure my personal joy of wearing sexy jeans again could also be the experience of millions of middle aged women, if they just gave my jeans a try.

With cautious optimism, HSN ordered 5,000 pairs of my jeans and allotted me one hour with a plus-size overnight host at five a.m. on a Sunday morning—not exactly prime time! So with no advertisement, no buildup, no announcement, and with me wondering who would be up in the middle of the night looking for baby boomer jeans, I went on air and simply spoke from my heart and my own personal experience. In less than five minutes, we sold all 5,000 pairs!

Someone up there was watching over me. I immediately called my business partner, who at six a.m. on a Sunday morning was groggy and more than a little annoyed. Until I gave him the numbers.

"We've really got something here," I said. "This is going to be huge! This is going to be a revolution!"

So what's the moral of the story?

I never would have designed those life-changing jeans if I hadn't thrown out the rulebook! And without thumbing my nose at tradition, I never would have found my true calling, my tribe, my new family, my "people."

As I suspected, my baby boomer sisters were out there, ready to be reawakened and reinvigorated. They'd been waiting, searching, and longing for all the same things I was—a way to recapture some of our youth, to get some of our "sexy" back.

Quite simply, the jeans were a sensation. Since that morning, we've broken every sales record HSN—and all of tele-retailing—ever had in apparel and beyond. I've become the number one fashion personality in all of tele-retailing around the globe, reaching career heights, levels of respect, and even an iconic stature that I had only dreamed of as a youth. And it all happened because I refused to listen to what society thought I was supposed to be and do at my age. I hadn't just thrown out that rulebook—I had built a bonfire and gleefully watched it go up in smoke!

Women were astonished at what the jeans did for their butts, and I was astonished at what the jeans did for their lives, their self-image, their self-esteem! I started hearing from women who felt renewed, reconnected to happier times and a self they'd almost forgotten. I was inundated with emails, comments, and phone calls—all wanting the same thing: *more.*

There was a huge reaction from women all over the map. They'd been waiting for someone to break the rules and toss out the mom jeans. They'd been told that they were over with, done. They weren't supposed get attention or even matter anymore. Moms and grandmoms shouldn't look sexy! It's not proper. It's not possible. According to the rulebook, as you age, you lose your mojo, your purpose, your looks, your place in productive society, your sexuality, your vitality.

Not me! And not you! Not anymore!

(Make that your new mantra.)

I was writing my own rules now and encouraging other women to do the same. If the majority of us bared our arms, grew long hair, showed some sex appeal, dated who we wanted to when we felt like it, eventually that would become the rule and the norm, wouldn't it? Or ideally, the new rule would be: *Everyone should do exactly what uniquely works best for her.* Of course, perceptions don't evolve overnight—not any more than change does.

You should have seen the eyebrows arch and lips smirk when it was revealed in the media that I was dating a younger man. One of the makeup artists I'd worked with actually refused to do my makeup anymore. "Disgusting!" he ranted. "It's not natural for women your age to have sex."

Forced to choose—throw out the rulebook or throw out the man—sorry. No contest.

Friends were always trying to fix me up with some silver fox doctor or lawyer—the perfect rulebook date—thinking that was the ideal match for me. I was certainly open to that possibility, but I wasn't closed off to every other man on earth. Finding someone younger was not a goal for me, or even in my line of vision, but finding someone to enjoy and love was. When I found him, I wasn't about to let anyone tell me it was wrong, especially if it felt this right! I was going to enjoy it for all it was worth. And, believe me, I do!

And why not? Whose business is it, anyway, whom I love or why?

Again, that rulebook of conventional wisdom applied to

older women is based on antiquated, flawed, and—quite frankly—cruel and prejudiced thinking. We're not an agrarian society anymore; childbearing has nothing to do with a woman's worth, and we shouldn't be put out to pasture as obsolete after having children is no longer an option. Puritan values never worked in the first place; prejudice is just wrong; and sex is as important to our spiritual well-being as eating and breathing.

On a personal level, the definitions of "done" and "not done" are seldom based on actual right and wrong—no matter what society says. So let's create a new ideal society for ourselves. We're the pioneer women in largely unexplored territory. You have to be brave, brave enough to throw out that rulebook and rewrite one uniquely based on you! It may seem daunting at first, but believe me, the rewards so outweigh the challenges! Finding your true, authentic self and purpose, and living your best years and most joyous life is priceless.

So, let's get started. Ask yourself what rules you follow because you feel like you should, because you fear you'll be ridiculed—ostracized, even—if you don't.

Take a step back and assess how these expectations do—

or, more likely, don't—dovetail with who you really are inside and how you really want to look, feel, and live your life. See—look honestly at what really matters to you and what you really want.

Now, for the fun part! I like to call it "prophecy fulfillment"—envision who you want to be, and then believe it enough to make it happen. Picture the you that you've lost, the one who is sassy and confident in a way you haven't been in years, and the kick-ass life she enjoys. What does that life include? Dream job? Travel? Family? Friends? Fashion? Spirituality? Love? Sex? (Of course, sex!)

And then, Do. Let's start by choosing one central area of your life that can be improved and then making a concrete, step-by-step plan toward self-improvement. It's a new age that requires a new rulebook—one that you will write for yourself. That's right—just for you! Finally, live it every day with gusto—Be.

As I rewrote my rulebook, I was determined to put a new twist on aging—not just "go with the flow," but also to see my age from a unique vantage point—something I would love you to do, too.

To help you get started, let me share a personal mantra

I repeat to myself on "down" days: *Diane, today is the youngest you will ever be. Don't waste it! Cherish it! This is the youngest day of the rest of your life.*

YOUR LIFE IS A SELF-PORTRAIT.

(Pick your palette,
lift your brush,
and start painting.)

Remember when we were young and life was serendipitous? Things happened for us—often in spite of us—as if the universe had chosen us to receive the bounty of its gifts, even when we were too oblivious, self-absorbed, or busy having fun to really appreciate how lucky we were, or how these rewards were shaping our lives. As time passes, it can feel like things happen to us, often against our will. Ugh. That's one definition of aging—the one we've been fed our whole lives. No wonder we need to be warriors in order to fight our way back to the heart of our joy.

Back in the day, we just happened to make it in life, because opportunities opened up before us without effort; now we have to make it happen. Bottom line—aging is not the free ride that youth was. As Congresswoman (during the seventies and eighties) Millicent Fenwick once said—paraphrasing the well-known Bette Davis quote—"Old age is not for sissies." We need to live the second half of our lives by design, creating our lives brush stroke by brush stroke. With creative power comes the ability to control and shape your life and your path forward into what you want them to be. Picture this: You are the artist and the rest of your life is a blank canvas just waiting for your inspiration and composition.

Does the picture you present to the world match the image in your mind and heart of who you really are, or long to be? Or has it been muddied and blurred by time, circumstances, and other people's expectations?

It's easy to lose sight of who we are and what we want. Believe me, I know all about it. I lost it for almost an entire decade. Let me rewind a few years and give you an example that was an incredibly powerful moment for me, one that taught me that I could hold that paintbrush in my hand, even at a time when much of my life felt like a runaway freight train.

ARE YOU READY FOR THE THREE-WAY?

A while back, in response to one of my blog posts on HuffPo, a reader quoted legendary baseball pitcher Satchel Paige: "How old would you be if you didn't know how old you are?" Thought provoking, right?

My husband forever changed my answer to that question one afternoon a few years before he died. My television career had just started taking off, and having been on his way to a career in pro football before he was sidelined by the accident that cost him an eye, Jim was pretty savvy about the dynamics of being a public figure.

At that point, Jim was dying, and we both knew it. While I poured all my energy into his cancer care, he worried about the difficult journey that lay ahead for me.

One day, he took my hand and led me to the three-way mirror in our bathroom. Yeah. The three-way. It was brutal!! He forced me to honestly look at myself from every angle, which I hadn't done in years! And I know why I'd avoided it, too.

I was in the habit of finding a way to dodge looking at my Yoda-chin profile (all three of them), but the harsh overhead light left me nowhere to hide. (Thank God this wasn't a full-length mirror. And there were no sharp objects on hand.) There was no denying the image that confronted me.

The woman in the mirror was middle aged, at best. Her face sagged, and her wrinkles furrowed. The light in her eyes was dimmed. Across her forehead, I could see the artifacts of way too many hours spent fiercely concentrating and worrying. Her skin was a dry husk, her hair a dowdy, thinning battle helmet. Not a great bet for success in either the fashion industry or on television.

Chronologically, I was forty-six, but brain-sucking stress had deflated me like a beach ball. Visually, I was pushing sixty and then some. How had I let "me" slide so far downhill, and how was I ever going to pull myself up again, even just halfway?

Luckily, I had Jim by my side to support me. But, as always, he wasn't about to do anything but tell me the truth, as he saw it, no matter how difficult it was to hear—he was a brave man and a true friend.

"Diane," Jim said. "Television is going to be a huge part of your career in the future. You can't put yourself out there looking like this and expect to be successful or believable. You need to take a long, honest look at yourself and ask that essential question: Is this the image I want to present to the world? Am I happy with the way people treat me and react to me?"

It sounds harsh, I know, but his attitude was: *I'm dying. I don't have time to be subtle.* If you can't be honest in a moment like that, when can you be?

And he was right.

Like it or not, we live in a visual world, in which we're judged on our looks. Maybe more in my dual industries—fashion and television—than in yours, but don't kid yourself—in yours, too. You're not expected to look like Heidi Klum, but you are expected to look like you give a damn about yourself and your appearance.

Beyond the superficial expectations of the fashion biz, on a personal level, this dowdiness I had allowed to shroud me did a terrible disservice to the person I was inside, the person I believed myself to be, and the person I was destined to become. This was not—at all—an accurate reflection of any of those aspects of my true self.

For nearly fifty years, I'd seen myself as a creative, dynamic, resilient, attractive, vibrant, sensual woman. In that mirror was a portrait of denial and the self-neglect born out of denial. As I looked at that disheveled, dilapidated broad, I said, "That's not me." This sudden clarity was a huge aha moment.

There's a great scene in *Fried Green Tomatoes* when Kathy Bates's character says something like, "Someone held a mirror up in front of me, and I didn't like what I saw. So you know what I did? I changed."

For me, it really was that simple. Change is a fact of life.

Either you embrace, and even steer it, or you stick your head in the sand, making it convenient for life to kick your ass. I never wanted to stop aging. (Jim was about to stop aging, and neither of us wanted that.) I wanted to renegotiate my age. To turn back the clock and redefine it. Somehow, I knew this was possible, even with no guidance, no antiaging rulebook, no spiritual GPS, and no icons to emulate. And the well-past-her-prime stranger in the three-way mirror made me realize that change was an imperative. I did not want to go on living inside this stranger.

So, yes, to pause for a "just between us girls" confession, that's right, I'll say it out loud: I got a face-lift in my late forties, and—alert the taboo police!—I'm not afraid to talk about it. Even though I lost a few judgmental friends over my decision—this was years before the Botox parties that are in vogue today—I didn't regret it for a single moment then, and I don't regret it now.

It was reaffirming and life-changing. It immediately took years off my appearance and laid the foundation for the hard work I would do in my late fifties—and for the positive results I would achieve. It made me feel good! There's an old saying that eighty percent of feeling good is looking good, and that sure holds true for me. And it was nobody's business but my own. It taught me to keep my own counsel and trust my own decisions—as long as I always remain honest with myself, rather than giving power to the negativity of others. Science is your friend, your best friend, actually, as I'll talk about in the Sixth Simple Truth. To quote my plastic surgeon when I asked him if my face-lift would hurt, he said: "To be honest, Diane . . . beauty can be uncomfortable." Fair enough!

"Mirror, mirror on the wall, who's the fairest of them all?"

Chances are that question from the gory tale of Snow White sent a chill up your spine when you were a little girl. But let's look at it from the wicked queen's perspective for a moment. How many of us simply assume that younger equals "fairest" and older means "crone"?

Is this the reality we want to inhabit, or just another example from that old, outdated rulebook we've already agreed to throw away? Now that we've empowered ourselves to do away with all that noise about how only young women get to be attractive, magnetic, vital, and sexy, let's embody the new reality we're creating, in which the fairest of us all are those women who project to the world how comfortable they are with themselves—at any age, with any body type.

The good news is that this fairy-tale beauty can be your reality, and at any age, too. Believe me when I tell you that the image you present is malleable and negotiable—twenty years ago, I looked twenty years older than I do today!

You deserve this new reality for yourself. It may be hard to believe before you've begun this journey, but with age can come confidence, wisdom, and a sense of power, which is sexy as hell. All you've got to do is create it for yourself. All? I know—it sounds like a monumental undertaking, doesn't it? But trust me: You have the power to give you back to yourself (as one incredible television caller said my jeans had done for her).

I know because I've been where you are, and I've laid down every stepping-stone on the very path that I'm sending you down now. I've taken all of these steps that I'm encouraging you to take. And I know they work because I'm living—and loving!—the results every day of my life. I plan to keep the process ongoing and refreshed for years to come. It's my pet project—me!

It didn't happen overnight, it took more than a year just to lose the weight and get in shape, and that was only the first step, but gradually, with effort, I saw myself—the me I always knew I could be—in the mirror again. Not the young me—I left her back in 1985 with the jewel-tone eye shadow and massive shoulder pads. The present-day me, a me who is actually a better me—a more accurate, refined manifestation of the beauty, power, and love I had inside all along. Like a little garter snake having shed her old skin, I feel bright green, supple, and slinky again.

THE FIRST STEP TO CREATING YOUR ✍ MASTERPIECE: YOU ✎

My transformation began with a brutally honest look in the mirror. And then, I had to develop an absolute belief that I had the power—and the right—to change and improve myself on so many levels. So come with me right now. Don't be afraid. I'm right beside you. It's time for your three-way.

Go to the most honest mirror in your house—the one that reveals the biggest portion of your body and in the brightest light. See: Take a long, hard look at yourself, just like Jim made me do, and answer these three questions for yourself:

[1] Is this an accurate reflection of who I am inside?
[2] Is this an accurate reflection of who I want to be?
[3] How old would I be if I didn't know how old I am?

I can tell you—when Jim forced me to that mirror at forty-eight years old, if I had to put an age on the woman who looked back at me, I would have guessed sixty-five.

I recently read about a brain condition that causes people to be unable to ever recognize themselves. Every time they look at their reflection, they see a stranger. I can relate. That's what I saw in the mirror before I took control of my body and my life—a middle aged stranger. Now, after the List, if I had that brain condition, and I looked in the mirror, I'd guess the stranger looking back at me was forty-eight or fifty-two.

In Nora Ephron's movie *You've Got Mail*, when Meg Ryan's character breaks up with her boyfriend, he asks her whether there is someone else.

She says, "No. But there is the dream of someone else."

That's what I want you to see in that mirror. The dream of someone else. The dream of you, as you want to be, as you were meant to be, as you deserve to be, and as you can be!

Take a long, healthy look in the mirror with me today. Then Do: Go back to your List and turn it into a strategy for creating a self-portrait that shows the world who you really are and that allows your true life force to become strong. It's about redefining the amount of importance you give to your chronological age.

Once you put your plan down on paper, you'll be able to break it into steps, figure out where to start, and how to assemble the team—(more good news, you do not have to do this alone)—that will help you to recreate yourself: hair stylist, makeup artist, cosmetic surgeon, dermatologist, nutritionist, or personal trainer. And no, I'm not saying you need to hire each and every one of these people, and if you can't afford to have a support team, your change won't occur. The positive results you seek are well within your reach—and today. And for those fixes that you need assistance with, once again, prioritize. Save up in the same way you would for a vacation or a new car, and make sure you get the best service your money can buy. Just like a home improvement project, you do some of it yourself, and then there are experts to do what you can't.

Start by picking one area that's well within your reach, your hair—coloring your gray, updating your outdated hairstyle, or taming the frizzy mess that has replaced the silky locks you once had as a young woman. (Think Cher in *Moonstruck* with her big makeover to meet Nicholas Cage at the opera.)

Be. I guarantee that you'll be encouraged—and gain momentum—and that the next steps will be easier—and fun! After all, what could be more enjoyable than becoming the woman you always wanted to be, and being your best self in a new world where you make things happen instead of just letting them happen to you?

All you have to do is truly want it—and I know you do, even if like me, it's taken you a little while (well, actually, a long while) to admit it to yourself. Take responsibility for your life, your health, your self-esteem, and your happiness. Get curious, do research (I did tons!), seek answers, and demand solutions—they're out there.

There's a dangerous undertow in our culture that can suck older women into invisibility, as if middle age were a black hole, antimatter. But it doesn't have to be that way. Not if we don't allow it. And just in case you need a little push, or justification, my research led me to the startling biological fact I already mentioned: before menopause, we females age half as fast as males. After menopause, we age *five times* faster. If that's not enough reason to take action, then I don't know what is!

THE FOURTH SIMPLE TRUTH:

THE UNIVERSE IS LISTENING.

(Don't argue when it answers!)

When I read Rhonda Byrne's book *The Secret*, I was blown away on almost every page. There are a thousand great insights, and the main theme of the book resonated with me: Everything that's coming into your life, you are attracting. That's the secret of *The Secret*—the Law of Attraction, or what I call "prophecy fulfillment"—but for me, there's another layer. It's about what we do with these gifts (or trials) that the universe sends our way in response to the energy we put out there.

I have a long history of getting broadsided by unmistakable Law-of-Attraction jackpots from the universe, but as I got older, I tended to place an obstacle course of doubts and questions in my own path, rather than easily accepting and enjoying these bounties as I had when I was younger.

Here's a prime example.

"THIS IS GOING TO BE FUN."

When I turned sixty, I had the world by the tail in a lot of ways. Creatively, I was doing some of the best design work of my life, working close to my heart, connecting on an emotional level with customers who completely humbled and amazed me. My jeans were an instant sensation, so commercially, I was enjoying a period of stellar success, and it was keeping me insanely busy. There was no gaping void in my life.

And yet . . .

I just wasn't as happy as I thought I should be. And that was because I lacked one of life's most fundamental gifts. I wanted love in my life again—not only to receive it, but also to give it.

After Jim's death, I'd participated in a series of half-hearted affairs, but nothing meaningful, fulfilling, or thrilling. One day, I thought, *So this is it? I'm going to go through the rest of my life without heart-stopping, romance novel cover-n-caliber love?* I felt a *sproing*—like a clockwork in my chest had just come unwound—followed by a rush of emotion, a specific moment in which it physically felt like my heart had broken. It was poignant and painful, but I realize now that instant of undeniable yearning was my shout-out to the universe: *I want this. I need this. I deserve this! I'm ready to love someone. Scary but true, I'm open to it, and I am saying it out loud!* Big step.

So many women I know reach the same place at my age. Widowed or divorced, quickly tired of the dating scene—if they're adventurous enough to go there at all—they accept the statistical improbability of finding a mate at this late stage in the game. Most women at that point declare that they don't need or want love. They say, "I'm not interested," because it's better to say, "I quit," before the boss says, "You're fired."

It's a crock. Don't believe it for a second when you hear a woman say that. Statistically, the number of women saying "I'm not interested in sex" does not sync with the number of women reading romance novels and erotica. How else would thirty-eight million copies of *Fifty Shades of Grey* have flown off the bookshelves? Clearly, the vast majority of women are very interested. They're just too afraid of rejection to acknowledge it.

Not me. I did want love. I do want love. I know the opportunities for women my age are few, but I also know that in work, in love, and in life, success is not linear, and in the second half of life, things don't just happen to you the way they do when you're young. You can't just go with the flow anymore—that automatic dating/mating game is for the young. Now you have to consciously open yourself up and release those pheromones with specific intention—and work it!

Jim always used to advise his clients, "Go to a private place and ask for what you want out loud. Trust that the universe will hear you." I remember sitting in my bedroom, high above Manhattan, thinking, *I have my own business. Television is heaven for Leos, so I'm completely in my element. Am I asking too much? Can I really have it all?*

Crowding in between me and the one thing I knew I wanted was all the second-guessing and reality-checking that we tend to do, but the pain of the yearning I felt was so piercing, so insistent that it drowned out my own self-doubt and all my fears. The one thing lacking in my life was that quintessential, take-my-breath-away romance. Would I really go to my grave without it? What a shame. It seemed wrong, so unfair. I took a deep breath, and with a huge leap of faith, I said out loud, "I want love again."

My brain kept right on telling me, *Don't be effing ridiculous. You're too old, too fat, too wrinkled, too imperfect. It won't happen.* But that didn't silence the desire: *I want that.*

Literally, A *few days* later, Attila showed up.

On a 2006 flight from New York to Tampa to do my show on HSN, I was bumped from my seat in first class. This almost never happened to me, and when it did, I had always been able to get reinstated to first class before. Not this time. As I made my unhappy way to the back of the plane after much heated discussion with the airline, I couldn't help but notice that I had been reseated next to a gorgeous guy. He was flirting with me before I got my carry-on into the overhead bin. And I was flirting back. (No harm in that, right?)

He looked like he was in his forties; I estimated ten to fifteen years younger than I am. The conversation began with pleasantries and casual small talk about travel and work, but we ended up engaged in one of those electrifying conversations where the intellectual and spiritual connection is as potent as the sexual chemistry. Talk about "contents may have shifted during flight"—I felt fairly rocked on my foundation, and it was pretty clear that the feeling was mutual.

After we landed, we wanted to keep the encounter going, but the logistics of his life and my inhuman work schedule dictated otherwise. All I could suggest was a quick drink at my hotel later, but the timing didn't work with his commitments. We kept in touch, though, and a few months later, we both happened to be in Tampa, where he lived and worked, at the same time again. Attila asked me out to dinner, and (always true to form) I agonized over what to wear, how much I weighed, how I should go get a spray tan and some sexy new underwear, and on and on and on, before finally settling on a classy, flattering, can't-go-wrong LBD (little black dress).

Long story short, he showed up at my door with champagne and strawberries, literally ripped that little black dress off my body, and threw me into a full-on, Fabio-on-the-cover romance novel of an affair. I recently opened up a drawer and saw the shreds of that dress—I know, I felt like Monica Lewinsky, keeping a memento of my sexy night, only this affair has since become a second-chance romance!

This new love affair was so different from my relationship with Jim. In many ways, I felt like I was in love for the first time in my life. It was thrilling. Dizzying! It reawakened all kinds of dormant feelings, reactions, and sensations—as a female, I felt alive again! I felt as if all of my molecules had been rearranged. I felt repurposed.

Now, years later, I look at this man across the dinner

table, and I'm still thunderstruck—not only has the love affair lasted, but it's actually grown into a relationship based on a deep heart connection.

"Did you have any idea that it would turn out like this?" I asked him recently. "What was in your mind when we first met?"

"I was wondering what kind of woman asks a man she just met to come to her hotel," he teased.

"I live in hotels," I said. "What was I supposed to do, invite you to meet me in an open field? Seriously. What were you thinking?"

"I was thinking, *this is going to be fun.* What were you thinking?"

"I was thinking . . ."

Oh, please! I didn't want to tell him what I had really been thinking at that moment, how my mind was a virtual blizzard of doubts, hang-ups, body issues, and negative self-talk:

Oh, my God! There goes my ultimate push-up support bra! Everything's headed south! Oh, God, he's beautiful, but one more inch and he'll see my bare—oh, God! He sees it! Why didn't I go to Pilates instead of eating that cheesecake? I can't believe I'm doing this. Can I do this? Everybody knows a woman my age isn't supposed to be doing this with a man who's younger than she is and has a flatter stomach. Huh-oh. What is he doing down there? Not the panties! I can't let him see the gray in my pubic hair! Why, why, why didn't I get that Brazilian wax when I got my roots done? This is insane. Where is this going? Why does he have to be so gorgeous and young? What will he say if he gets a good, long look at me? What will people say if they see us together? Does he not get that this is not allowed? Shit! Cellulite alert! Thighs in full view! Hit the lights! Hit the lights! Code red!

Meanwhile, this man had only one thought in his mind: *This is going to be fun.*

And it was fun! It still is. All that angst was a ridiculous waste of energy, and frankly, not worth the time it took to overthink the whole situation. I'd spoken my yearning aloud; the universe had given me exactly what I asked for; and instead of simply enjoying it, I was cluttering it with issues, most of which were products of my imagination and traditional upbringing—after all, my mother had told me emphatically that life for a woman was over at thirty, and at sixty-one, I was twice that age!

The love affair started out with a flash point of pure

chemistry, but over the years, it took a far more emotional turn and has moved very naturally from one romantic, spiritual, and intellectual level to the next. With happiness came a professional performance level that was off the charts. It's not a matter of "which came first, the chicken or the egg?" It's about how one essential breakthrough feeds other elements of life.

YOUR LIFE IS CALLING. DON'T LET IT GO TO VOICE MAIL.

It says in the Bible: "Ask, and it shall be given you; seek and ye shall find." Everything you yearn for is out there and available to you, but if you're afraid to acknowledge that you want it, if you're afraid to truly pry open your heart and ask for it, then you effectively close every door that would allow that gift, person, or opportunity into your life.

Speaking that desire out loud is a powerful first step, a catalyst for a cascade of change and growth, satisfaction, inspiration, and pleasure. But you can't follow that spoken yearning with a laundry list of conditions that the universe is required to abide by in order to fulfill it. Happily ever after rarely (if ever) resembles the scenario we originally envision.

Attila is not the man I had imagined for myself, and he is most definitely not the man any of my friends or family would have thought was an appropriate mate for my "golden years," but as a single woman dating in the minefield of modern love, you can't afford to narrow the field of viable contenders any further than nature already has. Age, race, religion, geography, the disapproval of friends and family, and a lot of other factors we may have seen as deal-breakers in our youth are not nearly as important as the fundamental questions: Does it make you happy? Does it feel good? Is it augmenting your life? Are you having fun?

This simple truth goes way beyond the dynamic of dating or even love in general. It applies to any desire and every relationship, whether you're talking about a blind date or your husband of thirty years, a career opportunity or a new book club.

Be willing to acknowledge your deepest desires and be conscious of the energy you devote to thwarting the universe's efforts to give you what you want. Make a habit of speaking what you need, then opening yourself to receive it. Don't preprogram yourself to think you can't get it.

Open the door, welcoming the fulfillment of your own wish. Open your heart, allowing for the possibility that you might be the fulfillment of someone else's deep desire. (Why not?) And open your mind, as well, to redefining "happily ever after" to be more in the present moment. After all, we are not talking about getting a date for the senior prom or finding a partner to father your children!

I've already looked deep into my own heart and had the courage to be profoundly honest with myself about what I wanted in my life and the likelihood that it might not happen—both as a professional woman who needed personal balance and as a real woman with emotional and sexual needs that I wasn't willing to deny or abstain from!

Even though I barely whispered it the first time, I felt like Julie Andrews twirling and singing from the mountaintops in *The Sound of Music.* I was sure everyone in the world knew . . . but they didn't. And when the universe gave me what I asked for, I forced myself to step up and enjoy it—even though Atilla was much younger and much handsomer than I ever thought I could catch for my middle aged self. Call it the "law of attraction," call it "prophecy fulfillment," call it "magnetism"—it works! There's never been a moment since we got together that I haven't felt deep gratitude toward the universe for bringing us together—and I never, ever take Atilla for granted—not for one minute.

So maybe begin like I did—with a shy whisper—or shout it to the rafters. Just be honest—no matter if you're embarrassed to admit it, even to yourself. See: Consider all aspects of your life: work, spiritual fulfillment, living situation, social life, family dynamic, romantic partner (or lack there of), and sex.

It's never a good idea to try to do it all at once. Do: Pick the one area of your life that's the most lacking or wanting, and start there. Synthesize your desire into one clear, simple statement. Go into a room by yourself with the intention to ask the universe for what you want. Say it out loud. And again and again. And know how much you deserve to create exactly what you want in your life.

Be: It's time for the good stuff: abundance, connection, recognition, pleasure! Whatever it is you want, it's within your power to have. Just like in *To Have and Have Not*—the

Bogie and Bacall movie in which she tells him all he has to do in his relationship with her is, "Maybe just whistle"—all you need to do is ask from an open heart.

SEXUALITY IS LIKE A PERFECT SOUFFLÉ: TRICKY BUT DELICIOUS.

(Get the right ingredients.)

I recently saw an article on MSN.com that supported my belief in the power of sex. It said, roughly: Lately there's been a heap of research touching on the health benefits of sex—it's an antidepressant, it's good for the immune system, and it even makes us smarter!! Sex is officially good! So why aren't more of us having more of it?

I know sex is a difficult topic for a lot of people, but you knew this was coming (no pun intended), and leaving one of your elemental needs in your past—especially one that is so directly tied to vitality and self-worth—is a great plodding rhino of a major ager, so it's important to talk about it.

I already shared the deeply personal and absolutely electric moment when Attila and I first became lovers, and I hope the takeaway there is the giant dose of *get over yourself* that I had to swallow in that interaction—letting go of my self-judgment and accepting that there was nothing I could do about the judgmental attitudes of other people was a big step for me.

Suddenly I found I was in an ongoing relationship that quickly became very important to me. It revived so much of my younger self, my true self, a happier self that was full of hope and confidence. I had gotten my groove back!

CHEMISTRY
⤳ IS EVERYTHING ⤳

I was never big on cooking until Attila came into my life. More of a hunter and gatherer than a creator, I either ate what was dished up or ordered in what I wanted. God knows I wanted to be a cook—I studied the Food Channel religiously, but I knew that I needed a master chef to be a sous chef for. I did not, on my own, know how to create a dish that was both nourishing and enjoyable.

Attila is a sensualist. In the kitchen and the bedroom, he revealed to me that there is great joy in the shared creation of something pleasurable from what is essentially nothing more than a chemical reaction.

Basic ingredients are essential, but you tweak the recipe to your taste. You have to have the ingredients on hand, understand how the elements work together, and be brave enough to experiment. Don't overthink it in the bedroom, just as you shouldn't overcook it in the kitchen.

There's great flavor to savor in every phase of life—the flavors differ, but each is rich and delicious in its own way.

A true gourmet has the skill (and the will) to elevate the combination of essential ingredients to create a sensual experience that goes beyond the fulfillment of a basic human need. Why settle for lukewarm leftovers or drive-through fried nuggets when—with a dollop of patience, a measure of self-education, and a sprinkle of get over yourself—you could serve up and enjoy an inspired feast?

The problem is, women have been programmed to lower our expectations as we age.

If you've left your childbearing years behind, sister, you are now the "sporting model." You can be that supremely luxurious, purely-for-pleasure woman who more than likely has her own financial foundation, doesn't need a biological or figurative "baby daddy," and isn't looking for someone to watch over her.

During my "lost decade," I went through a looooong stretch of celibacy, mostly self-imposed, that lasted for several years. When I eventually edged back into the dating world, the sex was not so hot. (And so not hot.) I felt like I was basically there to serve these older men's egos—and it was hard work! If this was sex, count me out.

I made a conscious choice to step back from the dating

scene. But first, I went through what I called Sexual Rehab.

Without the pressure of making my body desirable to someone else, I worked on making it what I wanted it to be: strong, healthy, toned, and energized. For me. Then I sought out specialized advice and gradually rebuilt a hormone mix that made sense with my lifestyle, experimenting with herbs and foods that are supposed to clear the mind, increase energy, and enhance libido.

What I learned brought me up short and yet explained a lot. As I've already revealed, before menopause, women age half as quickly as men, but afterward, they age five times faster! That means that aging is like a speeding train that's bearing down on women in middle age. If you were standing in the middle of a train track, watching a train barreling toward you, and you had a way to stop it or step out of the way, you would, wouldn't you? Well, there's a way to stop the aging train. It's called hormone replacement therapy.

Getting the right mix is tricky and doesn't happen overnight. But enlist a good, supportive, progressive anti-aging doctor who will work closely with you until you find the perfect combo that allows you to feel energized, youthful, and turned on again. There are "safe" hormones that have not been linked to cancer, and it's totally possible to make them work for you.

Walk—don't run. Do your research, seek out resources you can trust—on the Internet, in books, through your doctor, or by asking female friends—and decide what form of hormones will work best for you. I chose a plant-based regimen that's been proven noncarcinogenic, as opposed to other forms of estrogen, but that's just because it's the one that best suited me. Learn what's a good fit for your body and life circumstances.

Since my hormonal balance fluctuates, my doctor works with me annually to tweak the formula I take so that it addresses all of my needs as they come up—when Atilla and I started our affair, my doctor adjusted my hormone cocktail to increase my libido.

There are also herbal supplements that can increase libido—I didn't need my doctor's approval to do my own research, and through trial and error, self-improvement is there—and I take those, as well. It's so worth it. I think that men are very sensitive to the sex drive in women and that much of the time, when women are no longer approached by men, it's because the women are not throwing off the kind of pheromones that let men know they're still an eager, receptive sexual partner. So prepare yourself to be available, and then have all the sex you can!

Do not—do not!—tell yourself there's some nobility in toughing it out without hormones. I can't stand seeing a woman suffer because she's chosen to go through menopause the "natural" way. If you had bronchitis, you'd take antibiotics, right? If you had a headache, you'd take a pain reliever, right? So let's consider "change of life" as a physical annoyance that can be alleviated with a rather simple solution.

Kidney dialysis isn't natural. Would you turn that down? How about insulin or blood pressure medication? Oreo cookies? Diet Coke? Shoes? None of those things are "natural," and chances are, neither are your hair color, coffee sweetener, or contact lenses. Unless you were born and raised in a Papuan rain forest, you're the product of a chemically engineered, mechanically tweaked, anything-but-natural world, so denying yourself this vital, life-changing medicine in the name of "nature" is just not logical.

You want to know what is natural? Wanting sex, needing sex, having sex! Sex is elemental. It's a human need. Air, water, food, sex. We're built for it; it's our biology, and fascinating fact: Biologically, sex gets more intense as women age. (Ha! Finally an advantage over men!)

Sex balances me. It makes me happy. It makes me feel whole. I look fifteen years younger the next day, and (cue the Carole King piano riff), I feel like a natural woman.

Like a soufflé, our sexuality is fragile and takes great care, and the very first step is getting the right chemistry. Every time I nurture that—whether it's with vitamins, exercise, hormones, or a predate nap—I'm reminded how precious and worth it this effort is.

Mind-blowing sex happens on many levels, and hormone replacement isn't the only ingredient that helps to dial up the hotness. I can point you to the best lingerie stores in half a dozen major cities on two continents. I never wore lingerie until I was in my sixties—but trust me, it's a huge advantage for those of us with a less-than-perfect body. When I started dating Atilla, who happens to love lingerie, I began amassing quite the collection of lacy underthings. And, again, I never allowed myself to buy into outdated ideas about how this area of sexiness was off-limits to me, just because I was older. Instead, I reveled in how buying and wearing lingerie makes me feel (naughty!), and what kind of reaction it stirs up in Atilla (left to your imagination!), which is all the evidence I need to confirm that I'm still very much of lingerie-wearing age.

One of the most important tools at my disposal for maintaining that sexy self-possession is to stick to the regimen I started when I decided to take back my body and my life. I've made it a way of life to keep the weight off, maintain my muscle tone, and sustain the suppleness of my skin, even as I've continued to age. The more attention and care I give to myself, not only do I look better, but I also feel more worthy of love and sexual pleasure.

Still, there are times when—after a long, tense workday or a huge series of television shows—I don't feel like spending half an hour getting the seams straight on a pair of black silk stockings, but I do it anyway! I also toil over my inner self just as hard as I work on the exterior. Self-love is one of the best ways to age agelessly, and I strive to feel it every day.

✎ A COUGAR'S TALE ✎

Once I had finally made peace with my body and reached an emotional place where I was ready to connect with someone, love came to me out of the clear blue sky at 35,000 feet! And it just happened to be packaged in the form of a gorgeous, exotic, nocturnal, green-eyed, European male creature fourteen years younger than I am.

It took me a while to ask him exactly how old he was. (When he told me, realization hit me like a brick: *Oh, my God . . . I'm a cougar!*) I asked Attila if he was bothered by the difference in our ages, and he looked truly puzzled.

"Diane," he said with his rich, mysterious, utterly charming accent, "everyone cannot be born the same year, the same day, the same hour, the same minute. It's impossible. Knowing this, what does age matter?"

Oh my God! I loved him even more for that beautiful, sincere sentiment, but in the back of my mind, I couldn't help looking ahead.

It was difficult not to, given the often vicious response my relationship inspired in both friends and people who knew me from television and my HuffPo blog: "Don't fool yourself. You're delusional. It will never last. It will blow over. Someone that young will never stay with you, or be faithful, you moron. He's just using you. Don't lend him any money. Dump him before he dumps you. Don't be so arrogant that you would think to have a sex life at your age!" Most friends wouldn't even call him by his name.

The backlash extended beyond that, too, with some people going so far as to belittle me for feeling like I had any right to, or chance of, being attractive and magnetic. I soon realized that women were lashing out because they were afraid, just as I had been that first time Atilla tore me out of my little black dress. Luckily, I had already learned for myself that fear isn't reality, and so I forced myself to look at what was really happening between Atilla and me—which was the relationship, the romance, the friendship of a lifetime.

Realizing how shimmering and alive this affair made me feel, I have given a lot of myself to make it last, but I'd like to think that I would have done the same thing even if there weren't such an age difference between us. I knew the joys of long-term companionship, but I was also well aware that relationships don't maintain themselves, just as a person's youthful exterior doesn't maintain itself.

For a couple that has been together for a long time, as Jim and I had the luxury of being, the rituals of breakfast, dinner, and lovemaking become enormously comforting. Your lover's body is as familiar as his face across the table every morning. Because the history of that relationship begins when your bodies and faces are young, the changes are imperceptible and acceptable. You don't notice from one day to the next. Years pass. The history deepens, and hopefully it's a good history, because inevitably there's a day when all those imperceptible changes reach a tipping point, adding up to the bittersweet realization that the person in bed and across the table is an entirely different human being. I'll always remember a great Bette Davis movie in which she loses the love of her youth. He comes back to her years later in old age, blind, but in his mind's eye, he still sees her as the young, beautiful girl he had left to go to war, as how she would always stay for him. An artist friend of mine who's been with her husband for thirty years recently said to me, "It's not possible to stay married to the same person for thirty years, because it's not possible to be the same person for thirty years."

Long history forges strong bonds, but it also carries a lot of baggage. So in many ways, a woman in a long marriage is looking at many of the same challenges as a middle aged woman forging a brand new relationship. A while back, I wrote a fairly controversial blog post called "The Cougar's Survival Guide" for HuffPo, and that same artist friend and I had an interesting follow-up conversation about how much of my advice applies to middle aged women in more conventional marriages, as well.

I advised cougars to "embrace the energy budget." That's something we should all do anyway. Whether you're keeping up with grandchildren, a crazy career, a younger lover, or all of the above, it makes sense to optimize your body, maximize your time, and safeguard your health. Take those vitamins, sister! You'll need them!

I also gave some advice specific to those women in cougar-like situations, which I'm going to include here, as it seems likely (and amazing!) that this book may very well lead to a mass release of hot, confident, sexually primed women into the world! Recommendations included: "Be soft in private, tough in public. Fight your tendency to share and consider keeping the relationship quiet for the first year, and develop a thick skin."

Unlike silver foxes, who marry younger women—trophy

wives, whom they enjoy showing off—and even if you're a smoking hot Hollywood power player like Demi Moore, you're not allowed to have a beautiful younger male spouse without a lot of vicious judgmental gossip. So be brave, and don't listen to those snide remarks. (Listen to your heart only.) Tell yourself, *They'd be in my shoes in a heartbeat if they could!*

Cougars are well advised to learn the difference between "mommy" and mentor. I've often heard, "If you marry a child-groom, you wind up becoming the mommy-bride." Not necessarily true. Personally, I think of myself as confidant, advisor, and mentor. I love that he respects my wisdom, opinions, and advice as much as he craves my body. Yes, I do feel like I've died and gone to cougar heaven!

"Be honest with yourself," I urged my fellow cougars. "Does vanity play into your decision to get with a younger man?"

I won't deny it: my affair with a younger man does make me view myself in a more flattering, positive light. I feel hipper, edgier, cooler, younger, and, yes, more powerful. It always brings an inner smile to my psyche.

And yet, it doesn't hurt to be realistic. Chances are, a cougar may be having a brilliantly passionate encounter, but in most cases (including Demi), that red-hot intensity doesn't last. I don't say this as a buzzkill. These odds shouldn't make the experience any less fabulous. I'm just asking for a little pragmatism here.

I've been nothing but realistic in my relationship with Atilla from day one, and I've given him plenty of outs along the way. The fact that it's lasted for six years and grown into something much deeper and more integrated into the fabric of my life than I ever thought possible surprises no one more than me.

But, the best part about having protected myself with a realistic assessment of the situation—while enjoying every moment of connection and pleasure to the utmost—is that I have done a fantastic job of staying in the present throughout the relationship and just enjoying the gifts I'm given in the day to day—which we all know is an important part of savoring every moment of our lives, especially those most precious ones in the latter half. And for that, I'm eternally grateful—not only to Atilla, but also to myself, for having the good sense to get out of my own away and get the most out of what life offered me.

Which brings me to an important point: "Redefine

'happily ever after.'" Was Demi a sucker for thinking her marriage would work? Fifty percent of American marriages end in divorce. Everyone's a sucker for thinking it'll work! We do it because we believe in love, and six years of love is a hell of a lot better than seventy years of closed-off, uptight loneliness.

A writer friend once told me, "There's no such thing as a happy ending—only happy intervals and inevitable conclusions." The inevitable conclusion for any relationship: the couple splits or one partner dies. After Jim died, I thought I'd never believe in forever again.

On the other hand, the finite nature of the years we have here in this physical life only makes it all the more valuable, and with that in mind, I refuse to waste precious time analyzing or dreading the future. Today is my happily ever after, and I'm loving it. And you should too—damn right you deserve to feel good in your body, damn right you deserve someone who cares about you and makes you feel beautiful! Believing it is the first step toward making it come true.

Now it's your turn! Se. Do. Be. That's right, make your List: What are you hungry for? Take the time to think it through, then get to work developing the recipe. Are you seeing or feeling negative symptoms of your internal hormone shift? Has your libido sputtered out? Are you feeling distant from your husband or longtime partner? Are you alone and in need of a partner? Do you want love, romance, or just sex? Be honest, dig deep—no one's ever going to see this List but you.

Then, do your research. Be open to trial and error. But do try! Sex is too important to just give up.

I would urge any woman in a more traditional relationship to have the same candid conversation with herself. According to statistics compiled by CUNY's American Social History Project: "Despite the assumption by many males that women cease looking for sex, men and marriage after the age of 50, the fact is that, as one gynecologist put it, 'they remain interested in all these things until cremation.'"

The study goes on to quote some sobering statistics: Seventy percent of American women marry before age twenty-four. At age thirty, her odds of getting married are about fifty-fifty. At age forty, the probability is one in five. At fifty, it's one in sixteen. After sixty, only one out of sixty-two single, widowed, or divorced women will get married.

So don't ever let yourself feel like you're less than valuable, or desirable, or amazing if you go through a period of being single. And, even more importantly, don't ever be embarrassed that you want sex. As I've said, it took me years to broach this taboo subject and admit to my doctor that my libido had flagged, and now that I regularly enjoy the best sex of my life, I can't believe I waited so long to address the issue. Don't allow yourself to think that you don't have a right to enjoy your body, as well as another person's body, just because your body might not resemble the ones in a Victoria's Secret catalog—whose really does, anyhow? Not even the models—half of them are airbrushed. (Actually, all of them are airbrushed!)

Once you find the right balance for your own biology, you're a lot more likely to feel chemistry with someone else. But your sexuality isn't just about a man; it's all about you. It's the lacy underwear you wear under your jeans, even though no one's going to see them. It's about your own personal chemistry, what makes you feel most happy, most alive. And it's vital to who you are!

THE SIXTH SIMPLE TRUTH

SCIENCE IS A GIRL'S BEST FRIEND.

(Be smart about beautiful.)

In many ways, the concept of aging agelessly is an echo of the counterculture battle cry of our youth: "Hell no, we won't go!" We can't stop the clock, nor do we want to, because we're progressive—we've raised up some of the greatest cultural revolutionaries in history—but we are determined to create our own path and do what works for us, not trudge dutifully in the footsteps of our parents.

Conventional wisdom says that as we age, chemistry, biology, and physics are not on our side, but we're throwing that old rulebook out the window, remember? It's possible to turn science inside out and use it to age agelessly, which is now a common path forward, as attitudes about available resources are changing.

View self-improvement as a matter of self-respect. You don't feel guilty about exercise, do you? Or renovating your house, or turning in your car every few years for a newer model? So why shouldn't you apply that same approach to maintaining yourself? And feel guilt-free about it!

I'm not putting myself out there as a medical expert, just sharing my story, offering my take on the mixed messages, and hoping you might benefit from my experience. This is girlfriend talk, not a consult. (That said, I am a girlfriend who's done a lot of dedicated, self-motivated homework on this subject.)

ZEN AND THE ART OF
⤳ SELF-MAINTENANCE ⤳

Up to my whisker-burned neck in a relationship with an energetic younger man, I'm on a mission to stay energized and healthy—physically supple, strong, and attractive!—and maintain a deep mind-body connection! (Notice I didn't say, "I'm aiming to stay forever young.")

Recently, as Attila and I celebrated my sixty-seventh birthday, he said to me, "You know you're beautiful. Really beautiful!"

I said, "No, I'm not! I spend all my time on my imperfections."

It's true. It takes two hours of television makeup to remove every flaw and turn me into the Diane Gilman people expect to see on television. How am I supposed to roll out of bed and face the real me?

There's an element of this that takes place on the outside and an element that takes place on the inside. It's simply not enough to look good; you need to feel good, as well. After a certain age, beautiful has to emanate from within; self-love has to be obvious in order to create outer radiance. (We'll delve into this more when we get to the story of how I created my "super self" and how you can, too.)

My dermatologist, Dr. Misbah Khan, talks about the Four Ds of Aging: Descent, Deflation, Disproportion, and Distortion. (I would add two more: Dehydration and Dullness.)

"All this happens on a global, full-body level," says Dr. Khan, "but we appreciate it on the head and neck first, as we see it first. Most of these aspects of aging are reversible. The key is maintenance."

Think about that word for a minute. The dictionary defines it in the following way: "the process of preserving something; keeping something in good condition." I like to think of it as self-preservation.

I certainly believe that the judicious nip and tuck—surgery, injection treatments, or laser resurfacing—can be part of that, but in order to create real, dynamic improvement, the overall effort has to go much deeper, and it has to be absolutely personalized.

"I do everything based on the math of beauty," says my aesthetically attuned doctor. "It has to be right for the face and personality you're working on. It's like clothing, you know. One size cannot fit all."

Now she's speaking my language, and her take on it definitely resonates with my personal experience.

In my early fifties, my hair was falling out and getting thin and brittle; my skin was losing elasticity, dehydrating and gaining wrinkles at an alarming rate. I went and got hormone therapy (Premarin), and for a while, that solved some issues, but it didn't solve the biggest problem, which was my horrible back pain, and the fact that I didn't like aging, or way I was aging *at all*. As I reached my late fifties, added weight, joint pain, back pain, interrupted sleep patterns, disturbing dreams, and a lack of stamina made it increasingly difficult to keep up my hell-bent-for-glory work schedule. As an "I-don't-believe-I'll-ever-grow-old" baby boomer and someone who flat-out loves her work, retiring has never crossed my mind. I always figured I'd work till I'm 100, but the way my body was heading, I knew there was no way I'd be able to physically do that.

Leafing through a fashion magazine one day—feeling

old, lethargic, wrinkled, overweight, and frankly, dejected compared to the slinky models—I came upon an article about beating the clock, staying forever young, and how age-conscious people from global heads of state to seventeen-year-old fashion models were taking HGH (human growth hormone) supplements. I was instantly intrigued, and after doing extensive research and giving much thought to the pros and cons, I decided to make it the centerpiece of my regimen. Although I am well aware that it's not FDA approved as an anti-aging method, and it's controversial, it has absolutely transformed my life. But if you're considering making the same choice, you must do what's best for you.

Getting HGH was an execution of a desire to be able to retard the aging process so that I could do all the things I wanted to do for the rest of my life, but it's not a cure all. If there's one area in which I am a Dr. Frankenstein, it's how I've crafted a plan that works well for me from the total mishmash of stuff I've sifted through and researched. I remolded and customized my life with a dedicated purpose, and in doing so, I drew on discoveries in all different areas dedicated to improving the human experience, from technology and diet to exercise, herbs, and meditation.

ALL PART OF
❧ THE STRATEGY ❧

If I had decided against HGH, or if it hadn't worked for me, I would have gone on in a soldierly fashion to attack every one of the individual issues that I was able to tackle all at once with HGH: weight, skin, injuries, back and joint pain. HGH simplified and fast-tracked my self-improvement plan, giving me a tool that served as a huge umbrella for solving many problems. So far, taking HGH hasn't caused me any issues, but I'm very regimented about taking and working with it. (Key phrase: "working with." It's also important to note that I believed from the very first moment I read about HGH that it would work, so again, there's another instance of prophecy fulfillment in my life for you.)

When word started getting out about my doctor, he was being flown around the world by heads of state, sheiks, sultans, kings, Hollywood moguls, and stars. Everybody wanted to drink from this fountain of youth. But I know better than to approach it as a fad solution—and I was in for the long haul—it has to be part of an overall strategy that includes exercise, a proper diet, and regular cosmetic tweaks and improvements.

Yes! I'm not embarrassed to say it. I think it's fantastic that, through the miracle of modern science, I can get fat sucked out of my stomach and injected into my face! How great is that? I don't want to overdo it, and of course, I'm extremely selective about where on my body and by whom I have that or any cosmetic procedure done. I was encouraged to try getting a radical skin peel—called fraxel laser treatment—to refresh, but I couldn't go through with it. I had to tell them to stop—too scary! (See, I have my moments of fear and reservation, just like you!) People had been telling me to get fraxel treatment for years, but it sounded too painful. My doctor swore that stars went on the red carpet thirty-six hours after the procedure, because they looked so incredible. And yet, when it came time to go through with it, I was terrified. I knew that I'd be delivered to the procedure in a sub-basement parking area with a private elevator and that I'd be scary for a few days—the color of a roasted tomato. I just couldn't do it. But, given the procedure's promise, I eventually overcame my fears. Frankly, "it weren't nothing," as they say. The results? As one customer wrote in after I made a television appearance about a week later: "You glow, girl!"

I have to do it my way. That means standing up to pressure from both sides: well-meaning friends who feel compelled to offer an opinion and gung-ho salespeople who believe in their product. That would be one of my biggest pieces of advice for anyone who decides to make science her friend, too. You pick your friends carefully, right? Do the same with choices in self-improvement! When you're getting a procedure done, unless you're under anesthesia, you're conscious, and you're in control. Be sure to make your thoughts and feelings known about what you are going for and how you want to look. Be proactive. I've certainly spoken up. Once I was getting Juvéderm in my upper lip, and I told the doctor at a certain point to just back off! Enough! Basta! As far as I'm concerned, less is more—and I was very happy with the results, which looked quite natural.

I know I'm not alone in my desire to make science work for me—plastic surgery and dermatology are the fastest growing segments of the medical industry. It's not just vain uptown dowagers, and it's not just women. (A huge part of this fast growing industry is middle aged men seeking employment or mounting IPOs—they want to look young and refreshed, too!) No one on the red carpet wants to admit that they're not God-given perfect, but trust me, they're working their asses off and investing in their looks. I was just looking at a picture of Tom Cruise—he looks ten years younger than he did a year go, and wondering, Now what did he have done . . . face lift, Juvéderm fillers, fraxel, botox? All of the above? He's fifty, and he looks thirty-five, and not in a fake way. It occurs to me that I've had all of the above done, too, and that in the end, the sum of the parts is greater than the whole. All of those small, annoying, but essentially painless procedures took ten to fifteen years off my appearance, and every time I look in the mirror, I believe I am who I see!

A lot of people lie about "having work done" because they're afraid of what people will think. The prejudice and hypocrisy surrounding this issue are often vicious and always ridiculous. You can't control that; you have to get over it.

There's also the expense of cosmetic procedures; but it's not something you want to do on a bargain basis. That's definitely my primary advice about cosmetic interventions—don't go for bargain-basement cosmetic procedures. This is not like buying a sweater on sale at Macy's; it's the image you will present to the world for years to come. My overall tip is do what you can, when you can, and only if you want to. Don't see it as vain or selfish; see it as life-enhancement. Make it a project, just like you would any other area of your health and well-being.

You treat your car to new tires, regularly scheduled tune-ups, realignments, and oil changes. When your car gets a dent, you have it smoothed out. When the paint job gets a scratch, you have it resurfaced. In other words: maintenance, baby, maintenance! So why not your body and your face, too? Seriously! Don't feel like you need to ask anyone's permission to undergo a scientific intervention or improve yourself in any way. Just like everything else you've undertaken on your path to aging agelessly, this decision is nobody's business but yours! Don't let anyone make you feel otherwise, and certainly don't let anyone make you feel guilty.

Whether you have a thing going with a younger man or you've been married to your high-school sweetheart for twenty-five years, working at being the best you can be means you'll get more from the relationship. Whether you're constantly traveling and making public appearances, or you're performing every day at the office, store, courtroom, boardroom, or schoolroom—physical stamina and mental sharpness are a requirement.

Baby boomers, according to statistics, will live and work longer than any generation this earth has ever witnessed. Many of us will be out in the workforce competing with recent college grads when we're in our sixties and seventies. (And some of us will be recent college grads when we're in our sixties and seventies!) The rocking chair stereotype went out decades ago with ol' gray-haired Grandma Walton.

The overall result of aging agelessly is that people no longer rate me, or judge me, or dismiss me, because of my age. When they see me in action, they don't know how old I am—they just can't figure it out—so they just treat me like me. I feel more comfortable in my own skin than ever before. I can perform at my optimal level, and that's the long-term goal. It's an ongoing process, and it's fun—or at least, it is if you're doing it right—because it's one of those rare instances of doing something purely for yourself. I call it science, but honestly, to me it feels like magic. Science is more than my friend. It's my best friend—my BFF!

And it can be yours, too! Whatever level you choose to enter into of what I fondly call a "personal tweaking."

Taking this step involves another trip back to that truth-telling mirror. Make a list of areas you'd like to improve. And then do your research! Prioritize and make a plan—start small or be bold! But enjoy the fact that you have so many options available!

This brings me to another important point. While fashion means that having my "face to the outer world" is—and always has been—my lifeblood, my bread and butter, my reason for being, I recognize that it might not be all of that for you. If vanity means little to you and the cosmetic route just isn't something you want to focus on—and you want to put your hard work into a spiritual pursuit—nothing could make me happier.

Yes, I'll always be a big fan—and proponent—of a line I tweaked just a bit from Billy Crystal's *Saturday Night Live* bit. While he said, "It's better to look good than feel good," I say, "To look good is to feel good." But I know that not all women have it in them or find it relevant to put so much time and energy (and money) into their appearance. So for many (or most) of us, let's simply reverse that phrase: "To feel good is to look good"—a much more universal truth!

If you know that the physical aspect of my regimen just

isn't for you, I'm your number one supporter. And do you know why? Because you just took a major step toward looking at yourself, figuring out who you *really* are, and staying true to that self. So if you're working on your internal youthfulness instead of your external appearance, you will have successfully embraced the process of aging agelessly. And it will work for you if you stick to it!

The bottom line is: Educate, then activate yourself. Figure out what's right for you, and don't be afraid to invest the time and money in yourself. As that famous commercial says—"because you're worth it!" My personal and professional lives call on me to look and feel my best, and so do yours, though your reality may be very different from mine. Your goal is exactly the same as mine—aging agelessly and living your best, most vibrant life possible!

THE SEVENTH SIMPLE TRUTH

TECH SAVVY IS THE NEW SEXY.

(Stay plugged into the cosmic conversation.)

Trends come and go, but a smartphone or an iPad is always an au courant accessory. If your immediate response to this undeniable fact of life is "that's nice—for my kids, or my grand-kids, or my coworkers—but not for me, I don't need that," think again. The latest technological gadget is not so different from a pair of really great jeans. And we all know what the right pair of jeans can do for a woman! Okay, so I can't promise that a smartphone will make your butt look amazing, but it will do everything else jeans can do—make you feel sexy, youthful, modern, in the know, and engaged in the most au courant, up-to-the moment happenings in our culture.

As you remember from our opening section, technophobia is a major ager! Being tech savvy is just the opposite—it means staying open and connected to the conversations you care about. It's attractive because it advertises a willingness to learn and move beyond your normal comfort zone. It makes you available. It puts you in "the flow" and keeps you in the know! There used to be a saying in the fifties: "Be there or be square." They were talking about attending the latest rock-'n'-roll concert, but it could just as easily apply to today's ongoing, ever-rolling technological revolution. If you're not "there," you're square!

Sure, you don't want to be like the obnoxious jerk holding up the line while swiping through something on his new iPad and talking too loudly to a Bluetooth earring as everyone within earshot looks on in annoyance. And I'm not saying you need to be camping out in front of an Apple store for five days to be the first in line for the latest iPhone. But please be there (somewhere) in the mix, or you're missing out on the language of modernity, the cosmic conversation.

You certainly don't want to be the person who looks at her smartphone like it's a bomb because of a fear of learning something new. That used to be me with Facebook—I had to be carried into that particular electronic social scene kicking and screaming, but now I love it!

Somewhere between the two extremes is a healthy approach to technology that treats it as the helpful and fun tool it is. That's our target.

Stop thinking that your days are already completely consumed as it is and that the last thing you need is another way for people to get ahold of you (it's called healthy boundaries, my friends). Technology is designed to simplify and streamline life, and that's what we're aiming for. Think of it this way, learning to use GPS (another technological feature that I resisted forever!) takes a lot less time than getting lost does.

And trust me. I know of what I speak, as I'm the ultimate example of a former technophobe who had to be prodded and bullied and shamed into sending my first e-mail. I was sure, or at least hoping and praying, that the Internet was just a ridiculous fad—like pink hair—and would simply go away if I held out long enough. But of course it didn't. So eventually I adapted, and I now use technology—if not seamlessly, then at least competently and with great enjoyment in so many areas of my everyday life. I can't imagine living without it.

THE MAN ON THE
❧ MOON AND BEYOND ❧

Historians identify the major generational divide of our time as between those who were born before man landed on the moon and those who were born after. I might argue that baby boomers were more likely to have had their minds blown—and their lives changed—by watching the Beatles' iconic appearance on *The Ed Sullivan Show* in 1964. But certainly the fact that we were the generation that witnessed the televised moon landing in 1969 speaks volumes about the galactic changes and advances we've not only observed, but also actively taken part in during our lifetimes.

And it's not slowing down anytime soon, even if we'd like it to—so we should catch up! Fascinating technological progress is everywhere. Think about the advances we've seen: from the moon landing to space tourists. Unbelievable, but my mother came to America by ocean liner way before there were transatlantic airplanes and never rode in a car until she was twenty years old. My grandparents were convinced that the horse and buggy was here to stay! They'd be baffled by the changes in communication: from party lines to Facebook and Twitter. (Actually party lines and Twitter aren't all that different, but you know what I mean.)

No wonder we occasionally feel like we've reached critical mass in terms of technology! For a baby boomer like me, who has a hard time figuring out how to use an electric can opener, the speed of invention and the resulting benefits can seem like a tidal wave—I often feel swept out to sea, forever drowning in new information.

I was recently asked if I Tweet, and my immediate reaction was a sharp, defensive, "*No!*" That's always my default mode when it comes to new technology: instantaneous, defensive denial. My response to anyone telling me about some new gadget, widget, app, or software I'm supposed to assimilate is an eye roll accompanied by, "Do I have to? Eff. You."

But I don't stay in that mode because I can't—I know that! I open myself up to learning, just like I opened myself up to love and sex and success in my sixties—and I do my best to stay open. So, yes, I predict that I'll be Tweeting by the time this book comes out. Every time I feel like I've gone as far as I can (or want to) go, the universe nudges me to go a little further. I usually end up enjoying the challenge, and feeling very cool-girl and empowered to boot!

I find it incredibly exciting when another little window on the world opens up. As I've already identified right in the opening of this book, another major ager is staying stuck in a time bubble—enclosing yourself in a steel box—walling yourself off from what's current and winding up an "antique," yourself. Yes, there are times I want to hurl my Blackberry off the balcony, and Attila has a running comedy routine about my inability to control the stereo in my apartment (hey, it's got a lot of buttons—it's complicated!) and about how it fuels my paranoia that all electrical devices hate me (they do) and deliberately refuse to cooperate, like something out of a Stephen King novel. But all things considered, I'm a lot more plugged in than many of my fellow boomers.

Let's face it, many baby boomers are reticent about even using a food processer (that would be me!); you're certainly not about to find them on Twitter or Pinterest. But keeping up with the latest methods of communication and information keeps us vital, engaged, and relevant to the flow of the cosmic, universal conversation. It's the same dynamic we just applied to medical and cosmetic technology in the previous chapter. It can be intimidating, overwhelming, and to get the best results (as opposed to blowfish lips), you have to do your homework. I promise, the returns are well worth the effort.

It's not only important to keep up—it's also essential! As I've already said, one of the ultimate major agers is being shut off from technology. I'm sure you've come across a circle of boomers at a party talking about their cell phones like they're prehistoric man the first time he encountered the perplexing and terrifying wonder that was fire. Don't let that be you. Recently, while traveling, I suggested to my business partner—who's a decade my junior—that I text him my show results. His response? "I'm not sure my phone can do that. I don't know how to text." I was shocked. He's ten years younger than I am. "Have you been living in a cave for the last decade?" I asked him. I mean, we all learned to work the turntable and the VCR—an iPad's actually easier and more intuitive to use than either of those.

If you think about it, the very philosophy of social media is baby boomer friendly, geared for an aging populous that's more sedentary. It's incredible to me that we drag our heels about embracing it.

On the personal front, statistics show that families (and couples) tend to be more far-flung these days; geographically, we aren't always close to the people we care about most. Social media is the perfect way to keep in touch. And now that we're working longer and retiring later, we have to stay current in the workplace, too. Professionally, being able to dialogue with younger people—whether they're our subordinates, bosses, customers, or competitors—should be a major motivator for mastering technology.

Beyond all that is the fact that, well . . . it's cool! It's hip! It's egalitarian—young and old, we can all participate. The way a great pair of skinny jeans makes you feel and look cool, the latest iPhone in hand is another notch in the age-less belt. It contributes to a youthful attitude of engaged curiosity. I feel so, Gogo, as the Internet is called in flight, sending e-mail and shopping online. I feel mainstreamed, not left out.

Just think about the hottest contemporary heroines of cinema. Whether it's Ripley from *Alien*, or Lisbeth from *The Girl with the Dragon Tattoo*, these überbadass ladies are such masters of technology that it's like a weapon in their hands (and the hottest accessory possible, like the sexiest lingerie or the most in-demand Louboutin stiletto). A major part of their sex appeal is being so fearlessly tech savvy. They make themselves tech sexy—that's what I want to be!

I hate the feeling of being left behind, being excluded from the global conversation, falling behind the herd. I like to feel relevant, and yes, even cutting edge. I want to get the jokes. If you don't get onboard with the evolution, you're missing out on the revolution. I don't want to become part of the "dinosaur" generation. "Experience" is what happens when years go by; "old" is what happens when you stop learning and allow yourself to calcify.

Believe me, as I've probably made clear by now, I am not technology-minded by nature, and I don't pretend to be a tech whiz. I didn't even learn to send an e-mail until I was sixty. My standard pitch when I'm trying to get friends onboard is, "Hey, it's so easy, even I can do it!" And let me tell you, if they know me at all, they're immediately convinced that they *must* be able to master it, too. I'm telling you—I'm that bad, but for a good reason!

I'm selective about the storage space in my brain, so I don't latch on to every little thing, only those that will ultimately do one of three things: help me stay ahead of the curve in my professional life, amuse me, or save me time on a task I would have to do some other way.

I love texting! "Brevity is the soul of wit," as Shakespeare said. By nature texting (and sexting, if you're into it) tend to deliver the essence of a message in a lighter tone with a fraction of the hassle of writing a full e-mail or making a phone call. For me, less is more.

Texting is a great way to stay in touch and stay connected, especially in this increasingly hectic and fragmented world. Although, yes, it took me a bit to get the hang of texting, I now prefer it to phone conversations. I see talking on the phone as old-fashioned. Oh, and what about Skyping? That's my latest tech-territory acquisition, and I love it!

Given that my work life has me dividing my time between three cities and three continents—with more destinations to come soon—texting is a godsend when it comes to maintaining all of my important work and personal connections, no matter the difference in time zones or schedules. I'd be lost without it. No matter what your day-to-day life is like, you will be lost, too, if you don't learn to embrace the technology.

I can do so much more as a designer working with technology. Through HSN's website, I reach women around the world, and I know I will more than likely be able to make these new customers happy because right there in the palm of their hands, they have more brand information options than I could fit onto the racks in an entire city block of boutiques. Back in my old Bloomingdale's days, we couldn't have even imagined the possibilities that are reality today.

I'm not quite tech savvy yet, but I'm well on my way. I've gone from being truly technophobic to being technonervous; I'm not exactly scared of it anymore, but I'm not completely comfy with it either, so I can be a little cranky about it. That's valid considering just how tech-challenged I am. Attila recently got a lot of amusement out of how thrilled I was when I discovered that hitting the minute button twice on the microwave made it go two minutes instead of one! It only took me three years in my apartment and the mistake of accidentally hitting it twice to finally learn this little trick! It's a small thing, but—c'mon! Who knew?

One step at a time, my friends, and the first one is taking down your wall of fear and resistance and getting comfortable with the concept of not knowing but being willing to learn. Hang out on the learning curve. Don't be ashamed to admit that you need help, and don't let the smug tech-support kid on the other end of the phone line make you feel stupid.

I arrived fashionably late to the technology conversation. Okay, I admit that I had to be dragged kicking and screaming, but now that I'm here, none of it is as difficult as I'd built it up to be.

Or that's what I thought. But now there's Android phones—one of my brand's television managers has one that brings her to tears, *regularly*. She's thirty years younger than I am. No wonder I'm fearful. And *what* is Cloud—would someone please explain it to me? At first, I thought it had something to do with the weather report!

That's okay, though, because I don't work in technology, so I don't have to know everything or be a trendsetter ahead of the curve like I am in fashion. But I am totally confident that I can master enough of what's new to stay in the flow (or at least tread water), rather than feel like I'm drowning.

Even though I'm the designer and CEO of my own company, which will do $175 million in business this year, I don't expect myself to know everything. Modern technology absolutely humbles me! I'm not too proud to ask for assistance, so I do, often!

See. Pick one item of technology to tackle first—the one that you know will have the biggest impact on your day-to-day life. Start there and stay there until you "get it." Set aside the time to learn it and make it your own. *Do.* Relax and enjoy how your life has improved. *Be.*

I promise you that technology can be your friend—

maybe not your BFF, but at least your loyal helper. It's certainly made my life a lot more streamlined, and a lot more fun. (Without the Internet, how would my eighty-year-old cousin be able to send me animated porn jokes?)

THE EIGHTH SIMPLE TRUTH:

DARE TO DREAM.

(And watch your
dreams come true.)

Cinderella is an icon for transformation—one that has particular personal meaning for me. There's a lovely little song in the original Disney version of Cinderella: "A Dream is a Wish your Heart Makes". . . I've loved this song ever since I was a little girl, back when movies and dreams were a wonderful, much-needed escape from the reality of my dark home life and the (for me, at least) unappealing plans that my parents had for my future.

Dreaming came naturally to me when I was a child—it was a necessary coping mechanism for me to slip into a vision of myself in the future—but I wasn't dreaming about being a princess with a prince on the horizon, ready to rescue me. No, in my dreams, my talent rescued me. I was always a fabulously dressed, incredibly successful and worldly fashion designer who glided through the streets of Manhattan like it was my own personal kingdom. I dreamed that I was a shimmering gold thread woven through the beautiful tapestry of New York City. When we are young, we don't worry how it's going to happen, we just trust that it somehow will if we want it badly enough—and oh, do we ever!

Then, as we get older, we realize that there's no fairy

godmother who has our backs and that, while there may be a prince charming (or princess charming), he (or she) doesn't always stick around long enough for "happily ever after."

We are often told by our families, friends, and the world at large that our dreams are impractical, impossible, even embarrassing or shameful, and that we should get in line and do what's expected and accepted. That's why just one of the many instances of perfect timing in my life was the fact that I came of age during the wide open sixties, just when our generation decided to stick it to convention and dream up our own versions of adulthood that were creative, totally original, vividly realized, and pretty far out.

But then, to our surprise, we really did become the adults. Many among us became parents. We had partners, homes, businesses, and soon enough, our own aging parents to take care of, and it often felt like giving time or energy to our dreams—unless they had fully manifested themselves and were bringing us bundles of money and acclaim—meant we were being selfish, and sadly, we let them fall to the wayside.

But, just like that old rulebook we tossed out in the beginning—I'm going to give the heave-ho to this load of bull about dreams, too. The truth is we *can't* turn our backs on our dreams, because dreams are what we're made of—they're just as important to us as food, air, water and, yes, that other vital ingredient I always throw onto the list of life's essentials: sex.

We can't take care of the other people in our lives if we don't take care of ourselves first. Think about how worn down and burnt out I was before I remade myself and my life. This was me back then: low energy, out of breath after even the slightest exertion, racked by constant aches and pains in my back and knees, brought low by the worst self-esteem. How much was I really able to give anyone else back then? Sure I had a television career, but it wasn't anything like what I created once I started taking care of myself and seeking out pleasure, joy, and the challenge of renewed sexual fulfillment.

If there's one lesson I really want women (and men) to take away from this book, it's this: young or old, you deserve to dream; you deserve to be happy; you deserve to feel good in your body and the world around you; and you can absolutely make your dreams come true. It may sound improbable, even impossible, but it all starts with you. You've got to have the courage and the faith to dream—to be absolutely clear about what you want—and then, to be ready for the changes when they come, in whatever form they do—and they will!

These should be our golden years, not spent in a rocker creaking on a porch somewhere (unless, of course, that's what you truly want in your heart of hearts), but instead a shiny, promising time of discovery that find us out contributing to and receiving from the world—effectively sharing all of the wisdom and experience you've gained in your lifetime and enjoying all of the splendors that life has to offer. And, most of all, you should be sucking every ounce of joy out of your time in the here and now, because we are aging, and every moment is absolutely precious.

So, that said. Here's a little secret: If you're sitting there waiting for your fairy godmother to show up and make something happen, I've got (good) news for you: You don't have to wait. She's already here. She is *you*.

That's what I realized in the middle of one of my own oh-my-God-my-dream-came-true moments. Real-life Cinderella stories do happen, but they don't involve a fairy godmother showing up to zap everything into shape. In most versions (including mine), the protagonist makes the decision to get her act together and her mind in gear, does the hard work of change, and transforms her life, eventually rising from the ashes like a phoenix.

The first step in being your own fairy godmother: You have to have a vision—a dream—of the person you want to be and the life you want to live, and then break each goal down into manageable actions—again, your List—that will end with tangible results, which will eventually add up to your new dream-come-true reality. That's what the List is all about, and it's particularly important for manifesting your desires.

Sounds good, right? Unfortunately, for most people, it's not that easy. The problem is . . . after a certain age, we don't dare to dream anymore—we don't believe. I think we're so afraid that we'll be emotionally crushed if our dreams don't come through (having been disappointed more than a few times in our lives) that we're afraid to even try. If we were honest, though, love and sex would be right up there at the top of the list of things to aspire to in our lives.

I can't tell you how many women have fought me on the importance of such physical and emotional intimacy, in the same way that they've registered their disapproval about the bravado with which I've continued to put myself in the running to be considered attractive and live the life I choose to live, against all odds. Many women are so scared to dream for themselves that they will try to talk me out of dreaming, too. It's almost like they become their own lawyers, presenting the case for why their lives can't possibly get any better or ever be any closer to what they might actually want. I know why, too. Well, I can't tell you that I've never been the "anti-dream lawyer" in my own life. But that was the old me, the deflated me, and that should be the old you, too. It's time to dream! It's your God-given right! And no, there's no chance of our dreams *not* coming true, because even if they don't look exactly like what we first thought they would, we're smart enough now to identify the abundance of the universe when we finally do create it in our lives.

Let's talk about the essential partner of dreaming: entitlement. And no, I don't mean the negative definition of the word, which we think of as meaning snobbish or unsympathetic. Here's a story about how it can have a good meaning, too. Not long ago, I was at a very elite conference dedicated to successful tele-retailers. The extremely charismatic Madison Avenue advertising genius Donny Deutsch was a keynote speaker, and in part of his speech, he talked about how he'd love to be mayor of New York City. "Why not me?" he asked the audience with utter confidence. "It doesn't matter that I've never been in politics. I can raise money with the best of them. I know everybody who's anybody. I came up from the streets, and I'm still street-smart. I'm a great public speaker. I love my country. And working 24-7 comes naturally to me. So why not me???" He exuded pure entitlement! And I was so ready to sign up and work for his campaign!

Then he really brought his point home. "The most successful people I know have a sense of entitlement. It never occurs to them that they shouldn't have what they want, or won't accomplish what they set out to do."

That really resonated for me. You know, when I embarked on this journey of rediscovering myself at sixty, it never occurred to me that I wouldn't be able to age differently; I never questioned whether I deserved to create my response to aging which looked totally different than what had come before me or was happening around me at the time—just like it never occurred to me my jeans wouldn't be a huge success or I shouldn't or couldn't write this book!

Whenever I set out to do something new, I have a "who am I?" moment, which can be as unnerving as it is exciting. But I always trusted that I could find my bravest, most romantic, most authentic true self—the ever-evolving heart and soul of who I am. I went for it, and I totally made it happen!

I didn't feel like I needed to seek out anyone's permission or approval, either, which is good because I probably wouldn't have received it—based on the reaction I've gotten to my face-lift and my relationship with Atilla. But as I've already suggested, why should I ask for permission, anyhow? I deserved everything I wanted and more. I never doubted for a moment. I was entitled, and so are you. Never doubt that you deserve it!

Just keep repeating this mantra: *If I do believe, I will succeed.* It's a quick, easy reinforcement, and it'll work. You absolutely will succeed! It's the universal law of magnetic attraction—prophecy fulfillment, as I call it—and it's all yours to work with and enjoy.

You'd better have a sense of entitlement. While you don't need to get permission from anyone in your life or society at large, you may not get a lot of encouragement, either. Sure, once you start to achieve positive results, people will be all about your personal revolution and even take credit for it. But until then, there may very well be a lot of naysayers out there. Even though they're not about to admit it, they wish they looked and felt half as good—or performed in life half as well—as you do.

Think about it this way—I always remember how when I designed my first revolutionary DG2 jeans, I was told nobody wanted to see "fat old chicks" in jeans! And how my response was, *Who cares?! I don't want to see all of you old men with your beer guts hanging out of your polo shirts, either!* I sometimes think men have an easier time aging because they feel "entitled" to age in any way they please. So why not us, ladies?

Not to complain, mind you, but all the television ads I see aimed at baby boomers are focused on keeping men young—hair replacement, sexual enhancers, cholesterol controlling, even heartburn relievers! And they always show a slim silver fox with an obviously younger, blond, fertile, "hot," female mate. So as women of a certain age we have to fight a double whammy—ageism and sexism, a powerful combo . . . which brings me back to entitlement. When I met Atilla, I felt entitled to having full-on romance, super-hot sex, and lots of excitement with somebody younger than me who women (including me) find very attractive. If I hadn't, there is no way we would have connected.

A DREAM IS A WISH ✺ YOUR HEART MAKES ✺

Seriously, what are we so afraid of, anyhow? A dream is a wish your heart makes . . . and if your dream truly comes straight from your heart, with no doubts or reservations, with no negativity, and all positive energy, I guarantee that—in one form or another—that dream will come true. It may come in a different package than what you imagined. (As a little girl dreaming of fame as a designer, I would never have imagined my dream would come true through television retailing—which wasn't even invented until I was thirty-two—or that it would come true so much later in life than

I could ever have imagined—after sixty.) But to paraphrase the Rolling Stones: Sometimes you don't get what you want, but you do get what you need.

This was exactly what happened to me. Of course my dream morphed into television, and that turned into an amazing, life-changing avenue for me that has led to much greater success and so many more opportunities than I ever could have dreamed possible.

But most importantly, it connected me to my true passion, which I didn't even know I had before I did my first appearance on television—interacting directly and in the most profound, heartfelt, familiar way imaginable with all of you.

If I had turned up my nose at that first television opportunity (trust me, I thought about it), my dreams of fashion fame and fortune never would have come true for me at the level they have. Which leads me to an important point—at first, you may not recognize your dream-come-true. So you should visualize blessings, but be aware that they can come in odd packages, when least expected, and may not arrive whole, but take some time to fully develop. So remain open and vigilant!

For example, when I met Atilla, the thought of a younger man wasn't even on my psychic radar—I was looking for a silver fox, a peer, the man society and my friends and colleagues—and my own expectations—had dictated was "right" for me. So even though I was deeply attracted to him on so many levels, it took me a good while and a lot of internal wrestling and rearranging to recognize that this truly was the dream-come-true male who would reawaken and reconnect me to my true female self—the man who would give "me" back to me.

And here's another important rule about dreams: When I say never stop dreaming, I mean *never, ever* stop dreaming. Even though I've achieved so much that I dreamed of for myself, I've never stopped expanding my "picture" of what is possible. After I achieved success as a designer and television personality in America, I began to dream of conquering Europe, and I now appear on QVC UK and Milan—and next up will be Paris and Madrid—which is like my dream come true to the nth degree. I dreamed it, saw it in my mind's eye, believed it was possible, and it slowly but surely became my reality. Once you start with your first dream, that one dream works its way into another dream, and another, as they continue to build, expand, and wrap around one another—now that's the kind of self-fulfilling prophecy I can get excited about!

SAVOR
EVERY MOMENT

So here I am in my seventh decade of life, and for reasons I'll never quite understand—let's call it "karma" or "destiny"—it's finally my moment to celebrate and dance, and since I arrived at the ball under my own power, unlike Cinderella, I'm free to set my own curfew. I get to establish my own rules for "happily ever after." The life I'm living now doesn't look at all like the happily ever after I envisioned for myself when I was younger. (Thank God! I'm a lot smarter now and have a more flexible view of the world than I did back then.) And it definitely doesn't look like the reality traditionally prescribed for women my age—whatever that is; we threw out that old, dusty, outdated rulebook, remember? That's OK, too.

We're trained from the moment we're born to believe in

the traditional version of success and happiness, but there's so much wrong with that. For starters, the vision is so narrow, so limiting, so "cookie cutter," and when it comes to life fulfillment, there's no such thing as "one size fits all."

According to statistics, about fifty-seven percent of marriages last for fifteen years; only about five percent last for fifty. There's no reason to think of "happily ever after" as "the norm"; it's a rare combination of good luck, good health, and enormous effort. Does that mean ninety-five percent of us are out of the running for a fairy-tale ending? How monumentally impractical is that! Where would I be if I designed clothes only for size-zero stick figures? Or size-twenty-four divas? Just as gorgeous women come in all shapes and sizes, happiness comes in a variety of packages, and it's up to each of us to define it for ourself and, most importantly, to appreciate it when it comes by, cherishing every bit.

On a more intimate front, think of the happiness and balance Attila has brought into my personal life. He gave me (one of many) glass slippers and made me feel like a princess (my nickname, as it happens) while I was totally focused on being a lean, mean fashion machine—all work and no play. Until he came into my life and humanized me—I was way off center. He's a Libra—all about balance—and when I recognized that in him, I realized how deeply I'd needed it. When I'd dreamed of connecting again with a man, the universe gave me exactly what I needed. (Cue the Stones!)

He and I simply enjoy each other in moments of deep relaxation. He's a guy who makes it a point to smell the roses, while I'm on go-go-go-go-go überhyperdrive until I get sick and my "vacation" is a sinus infection that keeps me in bed for a week. Sometimes Atilla will very gently say, "Let's not talk shop." It takes a conscious effort for me to set it aside, but the moment I do, it's a pleasure-based evening instead of reality-based. He's the catalyst for that subtle transformation, but I'm the one who has to smack myself in the head with my magic wand and say, *Hey, Cinderella. You're missing the ball! Get out of the broom closet and onto the dance floor.*

That said, we've created a unique dynamic that works perfectly for us (which is nothing short of a miracle, as I never thought I'd find a man who was strong enough to deal with me, or my relentless schedule, but that's exactly what I drew to me when I finally, honestly opened my heart and dreamed it out loud).

Atilla doesn't fit the standard Prince Charming parameters in ways too numerous to mention—his age is the least of it—but he is as close to the wish my heart made as it's humanly possible to be. He revealed my sexual super self to me (more about the super self later) by showing me a sensual life without boundaries, shame, or embarrassment. This profoundly spiritual and physical connection was an unexpected gift, and had I been hung up on some definition of love as the "age-appropriate" silver fox I was supposed to go for, I would have missed it.

So dream a dream, please! You've got nothing to lose! Set the mood, and then let your mind and—most imporantly—your heart run free. Visualize your heart's desire. Think back to when you were a child and remember the dreams you had then, before someone told you that you'd better stop all that nonsense and get serious and realistic about your life. Well, you're a big girl now—no one can tell you not to dream!

Bottom line: Have the courage to look into your heart and find your deepest desire, visualize it and verbalize it—

dare to dream it—and then recognize the universe's answer to that dream, no matter how surprising the form it takes may be. Trust me: fairy tales do come true!

THE NINTH SIMPLE TRUTH:

TIME IS
AN ILLUSION.

(Seriously!
Ask Einstein!)

When Albert Einstein said, "Time is an illusion," he was talking about the laws of physics, about how time does not exist in the linear way we perceive it.

There's another, metaphorical level to this discussion, however. When we say something is "timeless," we're acknowledging that certain ideas, fashions, concepts of beauty, philosophies, and works of art have transcended time-based value systems and become universal, enduring truths. For me, it's a small leap from that concept of "timeless" to the concept of "ageless"—which is exactly how we want to exist.

Perhaps the biggest challenge of living AGE-LESS is to confront our traditional cultural definitions of time and age. Jim was onboard with the assertion that "perception is reality"; he believed that time was elastic, that time could stretch and contract, and that its only power over us is the power that we willingly grant it.

Think about it. Considering the vast field of variables that define our experiences and selves—some within our control, others dealt to us by life—age is just one of the many factors. It really makes no sense to sum up ourselves or our value (or the self or value of another person) by that number.

Age is the least relevant of all the quantifiable factors we use to measure health, vitality, and potential. Even more than that—although it's far more difficult to take a reading of—I would say that our attitudes are the most telling representation of our age.

For instance, I was "older" at fifty-two, during my "lost decade" than I am now at sixty-seven, and that has everything to do with how I see myself, treat myself, and choose to live my life.

As Bob Dylan said so eloquently in his song "My Back Pages," which I've loved since I was twenty-five—an age that is undeniably young, no matter how you measure it—"We were so much older then . . . we're younger than that now." It's almost like he (and I) knew what was coming for us boomers!

We're young as long as we stay supple—physically, mentally, and spiritually—as long as we stay curious, and most of all, as long as we stay open. Einstein also said, "Learn from yesterday, live for today, hope for tomorrow. The important thing is not to stop questioning." Sounds to me like he was describing a prescription for staying youthful— or rather, aging agelessly!

I'm not saying that sixty is the new forty; I'm saying that, on a fundamental level, both of those numbers are meaningless. And I'm not the only one who thinks so, either. Not that long ago I saw a Deepak Chopra interview on CNN, and Deepak said his chronological age is absolutely irrelevant — to the point where he refuses to acknowledge or verbalize it. *At All.* So he never refers to himself by the number of his birth years, but rather by his biological and spiritual age, which he says places him in his thirties. I'd say that's pretty easy to believe, given the insanely full schedule of writing, lecturing, and celebrity counseling he keeps up and how dynamic he looks.

I totally get his point—I too live by these same beliefs. Because our collective ideas of what it means to age are so personally and culturally restricting, once you say your age out loud, other people are going to put a whole bunch of outmoded limitations and heavy baggage on who you are and what you can do. I mean let's cop to the fact that we created this image of old age—when it begins and when it ends—that's now being shoved down our throats. We were the generation that said: "Don't trust anyone over thirty." Younger was better, and fashion totally skewed to our generation because we were this unstoppable avalanche of new ideas and attitudes that brought change. And we still are—so now it's up to us to change how we define getting older to take back our own power, to redefine ageless to AGE-LESS!

This isn't just wishful thinking on our parts, either. Antiaging doctors can test and measure their patients' reflexes and timed responses in order to determine their true, biological age. I did one of these tests not long ago, and my actual age came back as thirty-five. I'll take it!

The trick to aging agelessly is living agelessly. I rarely play the chronological age game, where I let myself get psyched out by outmoded ideas of the significance of my age. I don't even silently think it—it's just too limiting and would guarantee that almost every door of opportunity would be slammed shut in my face. Sure, I admit that I sometimes think about the numbers—recently, as I turned sixty-seven, my mind inevitably moved into fast-forward mode, and I couldn't help but think: *Oh my God, thirteen years from now, I'm going to be eighty!! Really?! Scary!!* But then again, when I was forty-seven, I'm sure I thought: *Oh my God, in thirteen years, I'm going to be sixty. Game over!* But of course, look at what sixty turned out to be—just the beginning of the best years of my life!

It wasn't until I turned sixty that I grew into what I call my super self and became a true Renaissance woman—not only a designer, but also a television personality and author—not to mention one of the most recognized comeback stories of the fashion world. Who knows, maybe eighty will be even more spectacular? I'm actually starting to reach the point where I can imagine that! And why not? Coco Chanel didn't design her iconic Chanel suit until she was seventy-two, and then only after having been disgraced and exiled from her beloved Paris for many, many years. Or look at fashion icon Iris Apfel—of the owl-eyed black spectacles and wild and impeccably curated high-low style. At age ninety-one, she's hotter than she's ever been, with a 2011 *New York Times* article dubbing her, "Fashion's Latest Pop Star." She didn't even do her first photo shoot until she was eighty-six, but it was with the fabled Bruce Weber for Italian *Vogue*. How fabulous! What an inspiration—now that's redefining the golden years!

When you blur the boundaries and stop giving credibility to the established and utterly limiting parameters of age, other people will too. For example, for a long time, the fashion industry has turned its back on older women, said we weren't relevant, weren't valuable as customers, and didn't belong in most of their designs, particularly jeans. I took that rather personally, and being a solution-driven person (a baby boomer concept) I designed my own line of jeans that were as sexy and vital as I still felt, only to find that I was *far from alone*. When my boomer sisters bought my designs to the tune of hundreds of millions of dollars a year, the fashion industry finally had to grudgingly acknowledge me and my singular vision for dressing my generation, but up until now, the same industry still hasn't changed its own attitude toward us—we are still the "forgotten women".

THE LAND
❧ THAT TIME FORGOT ❧

If there's any doubt in your mind that Einstein had it right when he said time is relative, go to a retirement community in Boca Raton and spend a few days watching *I Love Lucy* reruns, while eating white fish salad for breakfast, and playing cards all evening, discussing who just died and who's on their way. You want a longer life? Do that. It will be interminable. You'll pray for the sweet release of death.

And so I've come up with a new and original approach that I call "negotiating aging"—the true essence of AGE-LESS Sure, I have to sometimes make compromises with myself and the body I now inhabit. Sure I've had to make more than a few adjustments, add a few disciplines, delete a few meals. I was a wild woman in my youth—Studio 54, the Roxy, after-hours clubs, home at dawn, work, home for a few hours, and then out to do it all over again—but I need more sleep now. A lot more! I get myself to bed early, so I can sparkle and shine the next day. My nightlife is significantly diminished, but I have better focus than ever on my design life and my productivity through the roof. The plusses far outweigh the negatives as I structured my everyday life to AGE-LESS.

If we negotiate with aging it can actually offer us huge advantages. Believe it or not, there is a lot that's great about getting older (as I think my story and this whole book should be proving to you by now), and the stuff that's not great is largely within our power to influence, if not reshape and even control.

Time is elastic. I truly believe that. So take the second half of your life and stretch it out—expand it—make every moment intense and meaningful, and make every minute count.

My antiaging doctor believes that, if we stay on the hormone/vitamin-based regimen he's created and really take care of ourselves, reaching 120 years old, active and productive, is completely doable. I certainly believe that it's possible for me. All of my relatives live to be 100 without any of the interventions I've done, and all of my cousins who are in their eighties look and live like they're in their sixties. On top of this is the fact that I've also committed myself to seeking out the right food, the right vitamins and the right amount of exercise. As far as I'm concerned as long as I remain engaged and inspired, I'll see 120—no problem. Just thinking this way gives me a whole new view of time. I'm only halfway through my life! I've got so much left to accomplish, and the time to do it! And, as I go on, I hope to be reinventing how all of us think eighty and ninety looks, too. Hey, come on, I need some peer playmates! Cone join me!

Of all the factors that determine who we are, what we do, and the extent to which we enjoy life, I believe age is among the least relevant. Set it aside and see yourself as ageless—lift the heavy burden of that dreaded number (your numerical age right off yourself). Create a physical presence that reflects your ageless spirit, and open yourself to experience the world with fresh eyes again. Trust me, having the wisdom of more than sixty years and a youthful vibe is remarkably potent, incredibly powerful, and deadly effective because they never see you coming!

OK, my friends, we're ready to put in a lot of work, not just physically, but also mentally and spiritually. We'll focus on reshaping our bodies. We'll revamp our ideas about ourselves and our place in the world. And we'll get real about our "true" ages. Instead of going into some doctor's office to get a reflex test, we're going to measure your age, right here and right now.

Ask yourself this single question: *How old would I be if I didn't know how old I am?*

And if you don't like the answer you get, what are you going to do about it? Find ways to become AGE-LESS in your own life, just as I've done. To help you, here are a few tips for aging agelessly that you can put into practice right now.

YOUR TEMPLATE FOR AGING AGELESSLY

[1] Begin from within—have an inner dialogue with yourself and make your own List of what needs to change and how to make this change happen. Remember, it is just between you . . . and you!

[2] Learn to love the now—don't regret the past, and don't worry about the future. All we have in life is this moment. Learn to enjoy it!

[3] Create your own personal mantra. Here's mine: Today is the youngest day of my life—I'll never be younger than I am today—make the most of it!

[4] Perfection is an illusion—but aging agelessly is life's version of Photoshop. Use it!

[5] As for weight loss? You will find it impossible to quantify what you gain when you lose! Give "you" back to yourself!

[6] Healthy is not an age—beautiful is not a number!

[7] Is forty the new twenty? Not really, but forty, fifty, sixty (and beyond) can be the new AGE-LESS—simply be the

best you can be right now in the moment, and begin negotiating aging!

[8] *See* (your challenges). *Do* (form a plan for change). *Be* (the "you" of your dreams).

[9] Anything can change—everything is possible.

[10] My battle cry, my call to arms:

  * Never give up (changing, learning, growing, doing).

  * Never give in (to ageism).

  * It's never too late (to make the most out of your life)!

Sometimes shifting your way of thinking requires some major alterations—adding a new group of friends, a new daily routine, or a new mantra that galvanizes you and gives you a sense of purpose. Please believe it's your choice and completely within your power.

Throw out the numbers, just like you threw out the rulebook. Don't allow them to limit you, or control your reality, or even mean anything to you anymore. Change your mind, expand your vision, open your heart, ignite your spirit, and watch the world change its point of view toward you. Let yourself be free! Let yourself be AGE-LESS!

THE TENTH SIMPLE TRUTH:

CHOOSE TO BE THE REAL YOU.

(Become Your "Super Self.")

An apropos saying for this stage of our lives could be "saving the best for last." Like that gorgeous dessert at the end of a multicourse feast, we're just getting to the part that we really want to savor.

The same is true of this book—you didn't think I was going to give you *all* of the good stuff right up front, did you? I've been saving one of the biggest and best truths for just this moment.

So get ready to learn how to envision and create your super self—the "you" you've always dreamt you can be! Oh yes, she's hiding somewhere inside of you, just dying to come out.

For me, my super self first came to the surface in my late fifties, as I was losing the extra sixty pounds I'd been dragging around during my lost decade. As I slowly re-emerged, I had a life-altering realization: I had the power to decide who I was going to be now, how I was going to represent myself to the world. I realized I could and had to reinvent myself.

I started looking around for iconic role models, just like I'd done throughout my personal and professional life. I'd always drawn on fashion magazines, popular music and culture, and even street people. So where were my middle aged torchbearers?

Truthfully, there were none.

Mature women in the media spotlight were either over-the-top-bordering-on-campy, like ultra-glam Joan Collins in *Dynasty*; or a rotund, jolly asexual grandma, whose body is purely a lap for her grandchildren.

Help! Where was the me I wanted to be?

This truly felt like the first time in my life when I'd found myself with absolutely no guidance—with no media road markers or age-appropriate GPS. Up until middle age, there were certain prescribed, well-marked paths that most women followed—go to college or join the work force, get married, have children, be a wife. As much as I didn't ever want anyone telling me who to be or how to live, the familiarity of this multiple choice of options was comforting. Even if you wanted to rebel against it—at least you had benchmarks! Now, in middle age, there was nothing, zip, just a void! And it felt like, after a lifetime of driving on a well-marked highway, I was still behind the wheel, but suddenly there were no lines on the road, no signs, and no streetlamps—actually, no road! Nothing at all! I felt more than a little lost.

Since the woman I wanted to become didn't seem to exist, I set out to invent her, just the way I had my first pair of jeans!

I'll bet you already know what I did first, right? Of course, I made a list! I wrote down a wish-list for my new self (in the first column), how close I was (in the second column), and what I felt I needed to do to achieve each goal (in the third column). The first column looked like this:

[1] Lean, supple, toned body (I needed to finish losing the weight, and keep it off, but I was already getting there, which gave me confidence that I could look fierce and kept me on my exercise routine to make it happen)—I had to see weight control not as a punishment, but as a constant, ongoing process—a lifestyle shift.

[2] I identified at least one big key to my outward look—my long, lush, full, dramatic hair. (You may not believe this, but I didn't start blowing out my hair until I was sixty; that's how much of a Sixties flower child I was, but eventually, I wanted to be more age-appropriately polished.) I've found that my new sleek hair has become a huge part of my identity, especially unexpected in middle age. I

chose one powerful feature that said a lot about me and contemporized it.

[3] Healthy, clean, nourished, glowing skin (not much make-up)—and I tailored my diet to include a lot of salmon (omega fatty acids) and berries (antioxidants), and began taking specific vitamins to achieve that lit-from-within complexion.

[4] A reinvented, revamped wardrobe—believe me when I say, even for a dedicated fashionista, this was way harder than I expected; shopping became like walking through a minefield of fashion ageism. There was nothing I wanted that fit me! Nothing sent the message I wanted to convey—that I was still relevant, still sexy, but not trying too hard. Everything was built for a younger body—especially jeans. Totally frustrated, knowing my newly rediscovered "cool girl" image depended on them, I started designing my own, and that is how my DG2 jeans brand was born.

[5] Nothing says AGE-LESS like exuding joy! I work diligently at always maintaining a happy, vibrant, high-energy persona.

Once I'd made that most important list, I put the individual thoughts together into a complete new version of me. First off, I decided that, in many ways, less is more. Although I had been very bohemian in my youth, I didn't feel aging hippy was the best image for me now. So I did a complete 180 and toned it down while dressing it up—I aimed to marry class and the classics with glamour and a bit of edgi-ness in all aspects of my look and behavior. Usually, this meant choosing something impactful but simple, like a classic, well-cut blazer with a luxury turtleneck and my skinniest skinny jeans (jeans made it so cool-girl!), topped with skin that glows and hair that's always clean and beautifully blown out. (Admission: to be perfectly honest, it's a big, time-consuming pain to constantly tame my giant, Brillo-pad mane!)

Most importantly, I realized if you want to be beautiful past a certain age, you really need to allow your beauty to radiate from within—a happy soul has to shine through! My look was carefully curated but was also fueled by my spirituality and the work I'd done on my inner self.

And then an opportunity came my way that threw Project Super Self into overdrive—I had the chance to reinvent myself for television. This meant that I had the help of *a lot* of talented, visionary people to develop a television persona.

And so, in my late fifties, improbable as it may seem, I had many days when I looked and felt better than I ever had before, my super self was confident and supremely comfortable in her own skin. It made me feel powerful and positive—in control of my aging process, in control of my life, in control of me!

I was fortunate to receive on air coaching from the head of talent at HSN, Andy Sheldon, once one of the top talk show hosts in Great Britain. He took me under his wing and mentored me. It turns out that everything he taught me is just as applicable in "real life" as it is in front of the television camera.

One of the best pieces of advice he ever gave me is: "I don't care how pressured you are. I don't care how badly the show is going. I don't care how dejected you may feel that nothing is selling, or the audience just isn't there. I want you to go out there and have the very best time of your entire life. Be relaxed, open, joyous, laughing—never let the smile leave your face! Make them love you as much as you love them! Draw your viewers in. Magnetize them to you.

Don't you dare let anyone watching know that your heart is breaking inside if you happen to be having a painfully, under-watched show. No matter what choose to enjoy yourself. Choose to be the life of the party."

I have taken these words to heart, and both onscreen and off, I have learned to always keep my spirits and my energy up, my negativity compartmentalized—if I'm having a down day, I don't bring people down with me. I keep my negativity and complaints to a minimum. And it absolutely dictates the reaction I get back from the world around me—in all the best ways possible!

If you're doing your job correctly on television, you are essentially being a perfected version of yourself. For those hours, I'm tall (six-inch heels), thin (with a little help from Spanx), glowing (makeup), polished (hair stylist), eloquent (practice) and cheerful (mindful effort). I project myself as always happy to see you and be of service to you. And, you know what? I am! With all my heart! And it feels great! I love sharing my super self! It's just the type of self-fulfilling prophecy that I've been talking about all along. The more I love being that aspirational, inspirational version of me, my super self, the more naturally I slip into the identity of my super self all of the time—on camera and off.

And that's how, somewhere along the way in the past few years, there was a meeting—and eventually a melding of my two selves—my television super self and my real life, every-day self. My super self comes so naturally to me now, even without the benefit of a hair and makeup team, or a conscious effort to be high-energy and eloquent—it is me. I love that!

Now I almost think of my super self as my better half. I cultivate her, call on her, feel proud of her, and know that if I take care of her, she'll always be on my side, putting my best face forward, figuratively, for the world at large. The whole thing is pretty freaking amazing, especially when look-ing back at where I was at emotionally and physically during my late fifties.

Let me give you an example of how far I've come, but first, a bit of background: During the holidays last year, I shared with many of you in my HuffPo blog that this time of year can be a bit lonely for me. As you may have guessed from what I've shared about my personal life, Christmas dinner isn't exactly served up on a Norman Rockwell commemorative plate for me. Attila and I celebrate special occasions in our own way, but in keeping with the complex logistics of modern romance, he spends holidays with his teenage offspring on another coast.

After the hectic brain drain of a holiday season in the retail world, while friends and coworkers head out for vacations and family get-togethers, I take advantage of the calm, catching up on things at the office, enjoying the quiet time (exotic to me!), and loving my city—New York City—all lit up and festive. I do love my "stay-cation." But there are moments, I must admit, when I get a bit blue.

Last year, I spent Christmas Day loafing around the house and headed out on the morning after for a bit of retail therapy. Saks was crazy crowded with its after-Christmas sale, but I had a gift card: an excellent excuse to catch the "sales buzz." An unusual handbag called my name from a first-floor boutique area, where a single overwhelmed salesperson was struggling to keep up with the bargain sharks.

As I was standing in line, the customer ahead of me—drop-dead gorgeous, dripping in diamonds, decked head to toe in Gucci—turned to me and exclaimed, "Diane Gilman? You're more beautiful in person than you are on television. I love watching you!"

I almost fell over. This was a high-end shopper who

could obviously rock $800 status jeans if she wanted to, and she was tuning in to buy my jeans on HSN? I had to ask why.

"You," she said. "I just love you. You make me feel like I can take on the world."

With my day made (and that gorgeous handbag scored!), I worked my way upstream on the escalator, aiming for the shoe salon, but was sidetracked by a display of gorgeous coats on the second floor. A harried, hardworking saleswoman in a smart suit and sensible shoes muscled me in front of a mirror.

"I know who you are," she said. "You're just as lovely in person. Thank you for speaking out and saying all the things I feel like I can't say out loud."

Now I was completely blown away and so deeply touched. This kind of thing usually happens no more than once or twice a couple of times a month. Twice in the space of one hour? Happy holidays!

Hefting my bags, after having done some major retail damage, I escaped through the jewelry department to 50th Street, heading toward Madison Avenue to hail a cab. Suddenly, a car came up over the sidewalk and screeched to a halt. The back door flew open, and out jumped the cutest little woman with an ear-to-ear grin.

"Oh my God, Diane Gilman! I'm your biggest fan! Oh my God! I can't believe it's you!"

She launched into a blizzard of enthusiasm about how she loved my designs and had called into my show. She asked me to pose for pictures with her, her husband, and her son right there on 50th Street, which I did, my arms loaded with shopping bags and traffic roaring around us.

"I just had open-heart surgery," she told me, her eyes welling with emotion. "This is my first day out in six weeks . . . and I found you! You are my lucky star! You just made my holiday season."

"Believe me, you made mine too," I assured her sincerely as we parted with warm hugs and heartfelt best wishes and quite frankly, tears in my eyes.

I headed home, feeling so loved, so blessed, so honored, and so on-the-right-track for my purpose-driven life. I was becoming the woman I'd always wanted to be and always dreamt I could be.

That magical day after Christmas seemed like an amazingly positive omen for the New Year, a message from the universe, telling me to keep putting myself—my new self, my super self—out there.

Of one thing I am certain: Within each of us, there's a super self waiting to emerge—this better, more dynamic self we wish and dream we were. Yes, I have the huge advantage of having been able to develop my super self for television. But as I've already revealed, that super self isn't a phony mask that hides my true identity; it's more like a great facelift a week at a spa, or a perfect fitting jean that accentuates the positive and really brings out the best in you.

Because I have come so full circle in my life, I am very aware that my heart made this wish, dreamed this person I wanted to be, and believed I could be! Please trust me when I say you can do exactly the same. I hope this book has encouraged you to begin. If you take even one step of the many I've outlined in the book, you will undoubtedly begin the process of uncovering your true, super self, and introducing this side of yourself to the world. You'll become the person you were always meant to be!

I want to share one final list with you. I made this toward the end of writing this book, and I couldn't be happier with it, especially when compared to that tearful, angry, frustrated

List that kicked off my whole journey. Remember how the dislikes so out-numbered the likes? It was almost two-to-one! On the other hand, here's a list that I recently made on How I Feel About Growing Older.

NEGATIVES (ALL MANAGEABLE):

[1] Energy drop. (Take vitamins and get more sleep.)

[2] Easy weight gain. (Deal with it—maintain diet discipline and exercise.)

[3] Lots of beauty of maintenance! Ugh! (It is what it is.)

Now here's the other side.

POSITIVES:

[1] Gratitude: A heightened sense of the preciousness of each moment—every day feels like a very special gift.

[2] Can use my experience effectively (finally!)—my approach to life is so much more streamlined.

[3] Taking on the best role of my life
—I'm very comfortable as the
glamorous older woman. I "own it"!

[4] A sense of purposeful calm—so many
fears I suffered are behind me; fears
I would starve, fears I would be a failure.
(Honestly, I always used to tell my
friends I feared being that bag lady
out on the sidewalks of New York,
but instead of dropping a nickel
into my tin cup, people would be
dropping a nickel into my Prada bag!)

[5] I may have less energy than I did while
in my thirties, but I know how to use
what I do have so much more efficiently
and effectively.

Look at that—this time, the likes outweigh the dislikes by nearly two-to-one! How's that for a testament to just how well this whole AGE-LESS approach works?

Truth be told, I like the age I am! (I've never been more comfortable in my own skin.)

I'm not alone, either. A university survey of hundreds of thousands of people found that: after the age of fifty, people were happier and reported feeling less stress and anger. Sounds about right! Having been through just about everything and somehow coming out on the other side, it's a lot easier to stay Zen and remain above the cosmic blah-blah, no matter what gets thrown our way.

But before you go off to reinvent yourself and wow the world with *your* new-and-revitalized self, there's one final, infinitely important thing to say about the super self and about AGE-LESS: While my philosophy of always remaining too young to grow old is very much a matter of living and projecting a youthful vibe, it's really not about the external; it's a state of mind and the core tenant of what's actually a profoundly spiritual point of view. I truly believe those who carry joy in their hearts and gratitude for the gift of life in their souls will stay forever young.

Yes, we've talked a great deal about rebuilding and maintaining our physical appearance and health, our outer shell, but even more important is what we do about our minds, our essence, our heart, our spirit! At this point in our lives, the mind-body connection is everything. Check in with yourself regularly, and make sure your outward projection matches your inner self. One of the most important keys to AGE-LESS is transforming your spirit from tired to inspired.

When I look around me, I see that so many of our fellow baby boomers are angry—even bitter about growing old and don't regard the experience as having any value or enjoyment factor. They seem to feel cheated that youth didn't last forever.

God knows we stretched out our youth longer than any generation on this planet. So, get over it, already! I'm so grateful that at age sixty-seven, I'm healthy, active, challenged, inspired, and still learning . . . all things that I completely took for granted as a youth—in the same way that I took it for granted that I always seemed to have a hot boyfriend hovering around me. Now having a handsome, energetic, doting man in my life seems like a miracle, a positive nod from the universe, but back "in the day" I just treated it like an expected fact of my existence. I was such a spoiled young thing—I'm much more humble now!

At this point in my life, everything seems more crystal clear—more intense—more magical—more high definition. I'm a million times more grateful in my sixties for all of the glamour, romance, fame, money, hot sex, and career and life opportunities that have come my way—all of which were always implied to be out of reach to a middle aged woman like me. So every one of them seems like such an amazing bounty. Just remember, though, that I dreamed of and asked the universe for each one of these items before it ever came into my life. So I continue to dream up what I most desire to come next, while absolutely savoring and celebrating every moment of my life right now.

I believe that many people perceive me as younger than my chronological years not because of anything specific about my physical appearance, but because I project my spirit and inner light all around me—like a lovely aura. I believe it works just like a camera filter or good lighting does in the studio. It softens my image and blurs the decades—it's my cosmic version of Photoshop. For me, this is what I mean when I speak of "the mind-body connection," or having your inner and outer selves working in synchronized harmony.

Why do you think I'm still getting hit on at sixty-seven? (I find this fact incredible and slightly hilarious at the same time.) It's really not all about the physical. Although, yes I do believe that I look better than I have at any other time in my life, I really "own it" now. It's because I've put in the work to have that ageless energy.

It's like a riddle and a revelation all in one: maintaining my youthfulness leads to positive reactions from people (especially men!) that makes it easier for me to naturally feel more youthful. I swear—I love it!

We can revolutionize the process of aging and the perception of what comes with it and get our culture to embrace that old cliché that age is truly just a number. Believe me—I speak from experience—when I say most people won't care about your chronological age if you don't.

Get inspired by the personal mantra that continues to work so well for me: *Today is the youngest day of my life. I will never be younger than I am at this moment.* I'll bet this is just the opposite of your usual internal dialogue. True? Well, it's time to change that philosophy!

No matter how tired or achy I'm feeling when I wake up in the morning, or at the end of a long workday, repeating these words to myself always motivates me to be my best and look my best, which inevitably combine to help me feel my best, which of course is what we all want, right? To feel energized, inspired, connected—and good about yourselves!

Maybe you love my mantra, in which case, I would feel honored if you would adopt it and try it for yourself. Maybe you want to create your own. That's great, too! So long as you choose to be your own biggest cheerleader and cheer yourself on.

I would like to end this truth, and my book, in a deeply personal way by sharing one more lyric from the great folk poet Bob Dylan. It truly is my anthem, and the expression of what I want and hope for each and every one of us.

"May you stay forever young."

I truly hope for you, my friends, **that you will always be too young to grow old.**

ACKNOWLEDGMENTS

Mindy Grossman, the brilliant, visionary CEO of HSN, thank you for making Tele-retailing an aspirational place to be and thank you for giving me so much inspiration to climb to the heights of my profession.

Bill Zacijek—my business partner of twenty-plus years, thank you for being my "foundation," my "Rock of Gibraltar."

Stefani Greenfield, Desiree Gruber, and Hilla Narov, the creative "dream team" at my talent development agency, Full Picture, thank you for listening to my story and, against all odds and common sense, having made my dream of writing my book come true!!

Andy McNicol—my agent at William Morris Endeavor, thank you for your incredible support in making my story into a reality.

Jennifer Kasius—my editor at Perseus Books, thank you, not only for adopting my book, but also for allowing my "voice" to be heard.

Jim Rush—longtime companion, confidant, teacher, guide, and best friend, if only you could be here today, you would be so proud of what you accomplished in turning my life around.

"Atilla"—you've created miracles in my life, just by being you . . . thank you.

My HSN "Sisterhood"—without you, there wouldn't be a "me," thank you from the bottom of my heart.